W9-BUB-946

How to
LOWER
Your
PROPERTY
TAXES

.

R. Harry Koenig

A FIRESIDE BOOK

Published by Simon & Schuster
New York   London   Toronto   Sydney   Tokyo   Singapore

FIRESIDE
Simon & Schuster Building
Rockefeller Center
1230 Avenue of the Americas
New York, New York 10020

Copyright © 1990 by King Associates
Revised Edition Copyright © 1991 by Rene Koenig

All rights reserved including the right of reproduction in whole or
in part in any form.

First Fireside Edition 1991

Simon & Schuster, FIRESIDE, and colophons are registered
trademarks of Simon & Schuster Inc.

DESIGNED BY BARBARA MARKS
Manufactured in the United States of America

10   9   8   7   6   5   4   3   2   1
10   9   8   7   6   5   4   3   2   1   (pbk)

Library of Congress Cataloging-in-Publication Data
Koenig, R. Harry
    How to lower your property taxes/R. Harry Koenig.
        p.   cm.
    "A Fireside book."
    Includes bibliographical references and index.
    1. Tax protests and appeals—United States.   2. Real property
tax—United States.   3. Tax assessment—United States.
KF6760.K64   1990
343.7305′4—dc20
[347.30354]   91-10445   CIP
ISBN 0-671-74234-5
        0-671-73897-6 (pbk)

This publication is designed to provide accurate and
authoritative information with regard to the subject matter
covered. It is sold with the understanding that neither the
publisher nor the author is engaged in rendering legal,
accounting, or other professional advice. If legal advice or other
expert professional assistance is required, the services of a
competent professional person should be sought.

MAYWOOD PUBLIC LIBRARY

DATE DUE

MAYWOOD PUBLIC LIBRARY
121 SOUTH 5th AVE.
MAYWOOD, ILL. 60153

*In memory of
Noreen
and my parents.
May they be
happy forever.*

ACKNOWLEDGMENTS

To all of the people who have contributed in some significant way toward the publication of this book, my heartfelt thanks and appreciation. A very special thanks to Lucy Kraus, who wholly supported my writing and marketing efforts and who helped me substantially in getting things off the ground; to Dr. Richard D., who pointed me in the right direction and never stopped supporting or encouraging me; to Teresa Tritch, without whose article on property taxes this publication would not have happened and who went an extra mile to help me; to Fred Hills, for his inquiry and interest in my writing; to Ed Walters, for his excellent constructive criticisms and his superb contributions toward improving my original manuscript; and to Jeff Herman, for recognizing my original work, supporting it, and helping me with some very important matters.

CONTENTS

11
.
CONTENTS

PREFACE

The property tax system is a mystery to most home-owners in America. Most don't know how it works and many are not aware of their ability to challenge their taxes.

This book is designed to help you solve the mystique of the tax system and to explain, in layman's terms, just how to determine whether or not your residence is being fairly taxed. It also provides you with a proven method, which works in all states, for gathering and summarizing the necessary data to prepare a successful tax appeal.

From the book, you will learn:

- how the property tax system works
- how to determine whether or not you are being unfairly taxed, and if so, what to do about it
- what to look for to support your case properly
- how to gather and summarize the data needed for a successful tax appeal
- what to say and not say to the tax assessor
- how to file and successfully present your appeal

Forms and a checklist are provided to simplify your data-gathering efforts and to ensure that you don't overlook any important information. Examples are given throughout the book to enhance your understanding of what needs to be done and how to do it.

When you've completed the book and properly collected and summarized the data for your appeal, you'll be able to present information effectively to your local tax assessor. If your assessor doesn't agree with your conclusions, you will know how to proceed with an appeal and what you'll need to be successful at that level.

INTRODUCTION

Most people don't know that it's possible to reduce the property taxes on their personal residence. In fact, not only is it possible, but it is relatively easy, contrary to what you might imagine.

But it isn't quite as easy as walking into the tax assessor's office, informing him or her that you think your taxes are outrageously high, and expecting a reduction on the spot. On the other hand, if you are armed with the right information, i.e., data that properly supports your demand, and you take the proven approach described in this book, you'll have an excellent chance of getting the reduction that you think you deserve. The time you spend gathering the necessary information and preparing your appeal, usually between six and ten hours, will be well worth your effort.

Not every homeowner can get a property tax reduction—because his or her taxes may not be out of line. But studies have shown that in the case of about 60 percent of America's households, there is sufficient evidence to warrant a tax reduction. There are a wide variety of reasons that could help to justify one. For example, there might be arithmetic errors in the tax records, the age of your residence may be grossly incorrect in the records, you may own a one-story house but be taxed for a two-story house, the dimensions of your land may be wrong in the tax records, or you may not have been given an exemption (as a veteran, for example) to which you are entitled.

It has been said that nothing is certain except

death and taxes. When people use this phrase, they usually are referring to their federal income taxes. Why is it that more people complain about their federal income taxes than about their local taxes—the property taxes on their residence?

Perhaps it's because the federal government takes a chunk of our hard-earned money out of each paycheck. Local governments are much more clever. They decide how much we owe, but leave it up to the mortgage company to conceal our tax payment as part of a lump-sum, monthly house payment. It's so carefully hidden that we hardly even realize we're paying it.

Another reason we don't complain about our property tax is that most people don't understand the process. We may even think it's not worth the trouble to fight these taxes because our perception is that we can't win anyway. Not true!

According to the International Association of Assessing Officers, an organization dedicated to the proper valuation of property for assessment purposes, more than half of the homeowners who protest their assessments get them reduced.

According to a study of Rochester, N.Y., taxpayers by the Lincoln Institute of Land Policy, in Cambridge, Mass., only 2 percent of homeowners carried their complaints beyond the local assessor. Of those who did, about half succeeded in winning some relief—an average reduction of 8 percent in assessed value. Those who took their cases to court got an average reduction of 13 percent, and those who went to the Supreme Court got their assessments rolled back an average of 37 percent. You probably won't need to take your appeal that far, but why shouldn't you be one of those homeowners who have questioned their taxes and won?

By purchasing this book, you have shown that you are willing to learn the process and analyze your prospects for lowering the property tax on your home. Even if you have put forth the effort and discover that there are no errors in your tax records, or that a comparison to other properties like yours shows that you are being fairly taxed, you won't come up empty-handed. You will understand the tax process and be equipped to prepare a tax appeal on your next residence. In addition, you'll feel satisfied that your taxes are fair and that you have analyzed them properly.

But keep in mind, you have an excellent opportunity to get your taxes lowered—a better than 50-percent chance. Remember also that any reduction you do get will save you money for many years to come, not just the current year.

Before we begin, let's briefly examine the content and purpose of each chapter in the book. The following outline provides an overview of the book, the tax appeal process, and the recommended procedures for challenging your taxes.

Chapter 1—The Process for Challenging Your Taxes—Outlines an eight-step process that guides you through the analysis, data gathering, case preparation, and appeal procedures involved in challenging your property taxes.

Chapter 2—How Property Taxes Are Levied—Summarizes how and why taxes are levied and collected in a taxing municipality. It explains such things as the appraisal process, tax adjustments, and the details of a tax bill.

Chapter 3—How the Tax Appeal Process Works—Summarizes the tax appeal process and the filing procedures required to make a formal or informal tax appeal.

Chapter 4—How Property Value Is Determined—Defines the various approaches used to establish the value of a property and explains what approaches are most effective and which are used for residential properties.

Chapter 5—Adjustments to Value—Describes the various types of adjustments to property values that are required when comparing your property to similar properties. These adjustments are necessary to compensate for any differences, such as age, location, physical condition, etc., between properties.

Chapter 6—Other Reasons to Challenge Your Property Tax—Defines and explains the meaning of illegal and unequal assessments and provides lists of the types of situations that may exist that would justify a tax reduction.

Chapter 7—Researching Your Tax Appeal—Describes the exact procedures to follow in gathering and organizing data for a tax appeal. Examples of summarized data are included.

Chapter 8—Key Points to Remember in Preparing Your Appeal—Provides helpful hints and tips on how to present your appeal most effectively.

Chapter 9—Presenting Your Appeal—Outlines the recommended approach to use when presenting your appeal to the tax assessor or review board.

Chapter 10—Sample Cases—Examples of the entire process of appealing your taxes—from analyzing your situation, gathering data, summarizing and organizing it in an effective manner, and winning your appeal. A step-by-step example, with illustrations, is shown for a single family house and for a condominium.

Chapter 11—Enjoying Your Win—Addresses the efforts you have put forth and the results.

Appendix A—Checklist for Appealing Your Property Taxes—A checklist to be used by the homeowner to verify that all reasons for a tax reduction have been explored.

Appendix B—Forms—Blank forms that you can use to summarize your tax appeal data.

Glossary—A detailed summary of terms used in the book.

References—A list of additional reading material that can help you understand the tax appeal process.

As you read through the book you'll encounter a number of terms that you may not be familiar with. I will briefly define them for you as they are introduced, but I've also provided a more detailed explanation in the Glossary.

Now that you have an ample overview of the contents of the book, let's begin your education in analyzing, collecting, organizing, and presenting the data for your tax appeal.

CHAPTER 1

.

The Process for Challenging Your Taxes

Let's begin by examining the process for challenging your property taxes. This section will provide you with an overview of the complete process. Once you understand the overall process, you can more easily learn the step-by-step details of what must be accomplished to get your taxes reduced. The process has been divided into eight steps as follows:

1. Understand the process. (See Chapters 1–3.)
2. Know the valid reasons for which you can appeal your taxes. (See Chapters 4–6.)
3. Gather information to determine whether or not you should challenge your taxes. (See Chapter 7.)
4. Analyze the data you have collected. (See Chapters 7 & 8.)
5. Prepare your documentation for an appeal. (See Chapters 7 & 8.)
6. Discuss your case with the local assessor. (See Chapter 9.)
7. Present your case to the tax review board. (See Chapter 9.)
8. Appeal to a higher court. (See Chapter 9.)

Don't worry, in most cases, you'll never get to steps seven and eight. If you have properly prepared and presented your case to the assessor, you won't have an opportunity to meet the review board—you will have won your case.

Let's proceed with an explanation of each step.

Step 1—Understand the process.

Before you delve into the details of how to prepare a tax appeal, it is important for you to understand how your tax system works and the assumptions behind the property tax system. In Chapter 2, we'll look at a model property tax system to show you how taxes are administered.

Step 2—Know the valid reasons for which you can appeal your taxes.

You will be appealing your taxes based on one of the following:

1. The assessed value of your property is too high.

Since your property taxes are based upon the assessed value of your property, it is important to determine whether or not this value is fair. The value that the tax assessor establishes for your property (the assessed value) is based on its market value or a fraction thereof as determined by the law in your state.

One of the most common and important reasons to appeal your taxes is that the property is overvalued and therefore, overassessed, compared to comparable houses in your neighborhood. The tax laws are based on an assumption of fair and equal assessments. If your assessment is too high, you are paying more taxes than you should have to.

2. An illegal assessment.

One example of an illegal assessment is a property assessed at more than the legal percentage. In some states, the assessment is based on a legally established percentage of its market value (or some other similar value). For example, let's assume that this figure is 50 percent. If the market value of your property is $100,000 and the assessed value is set at $75,000 (75 percent of its market value), you are being overtaxed. It should be assessed at $50,000 (50%) in this case.

Sometimes these percentages are applied incorrectly, and if you find that your home is assessed at a higher percentage of its market value than the law allows, you're entitled to have your taxes lowered. (See Chapter 6 for more details.)

3. An unequal assessment.

An unequal assessment is property that is over assessed at more than its market value. For example, suppose that you recently purchased your home for $100,000, but it is assessed at $130,000. The assessed value, if it is required by law to be set at market value, should be reduced to $100,000. As compared to an illegal assessment, here we are looking at property that has been assessed above its market value instead of in comparison to a percentage that has been set by law. In this case, assessments are intended to be equivalent to market value.

4. An error in your tax records.

Often you can find errors in your tax records that qualify you for a tax reduction. These may include such things as mathematical errors, or errors in recording the correct size of your house or lot. Two typical errors are that the age of the building is incorrect on the assessor's tax record (called the property record card), or there's an arithmetic error in the computation of the building size. More about all of this later (see pages 74–79)!

Step 3—Gather information to determine whether or not you should challenge your taxes.

This entails examining your tax records in the local assessor's office, to insure that the data on which your assessment is based is accurate and complete. It also involves searching for houses in your neighborhood that are comparable in size, style, and construction to your property. See Chapter 7 for more details.

Step 4—Analyze the data you have collected.

Here you will fill out some forms that will help you evaluate properties comparable to yours using the market and equity analysis approaches. You will also be looking for errors on your property record card, and for illegal or unequal assessments, or exemptions to which you are entitled but which do not appear in the tax records.

If you determine that you have a valid basis for a tax appeal, then you will organize your data for that appeal.

Step 5—Prepare your documentation for an appeal.

You will already have completed the forms needed to determine the value of your property versus the comparable properties. Now, you'll prepare this to present to your assessor. Next you will want to compile a list of all errors found and indicate what is wrong.

In addition, you will be making a list of any illegal assessments or unequal assessments (e.g., a comparison of assessed values) or any exemption to which you are entitled but have not received.

At the end of your documentation, you should always calculate and state an amount to which you want your assessed valuation lowered and your reasons for choosing that value. In other words, you want to go to the meeting with your assessor with a figure in mind. It is important for you to present that figure in writing as a conclusion to your documentation. If you don't, the assessor may pick an adjusted tax amount that is unsatisfactory to you.

Step 6—Discuss your case with the local assessor.

Contact your tax assessor by telephone, arrange for an informal meeting, and present your case. Provide the assessor with a copy of your documentation. You'll review it with him/her in an informal, nonthreatening, polite manner. Remember that you are well prepared, and as a result of this, you will be convincing and persuasive. Very likely you will have a good chance to win your case. The assessor will respect you for what you have done because you have presented him or her with facts, not solely your opinion that your taxes are too high. Always conclude your meeting by presenting the value you have calculated for the assessed value on your property.

If the assessor does not agree with your conclusions, your next recourse is to present your case to the tax review board.

Step 7—Present your case to the tax review board.

The board may be referred to by some other name, such as the County Board of Taxation, the Board of Equalization, the Board of Tax Adjustment, the County Board of Supervisors, or some similar name. Some of these boards are elected, others are appointed.

The function of the review board is to hear your case objectively and render a decision. Often, but not always, the hearing is conducted in a courtroom. There will be legal formalities to follow, but you can find out what these are by attending a review board session or by contacting your assessor or the review board administrative office.

Step 8—Appeal to a higher court.

There may be a valid reason for you to appeal to a higher court, such as an agency, a specialized tax court, an appeals court, or the Supreme Court in your state. At this point, you would probably want to hire an attorney to represent you. Very few homeowner cases would ever reach this level.

Hopefully, the information presented to this point has provided you with a useful overview and a general understanding of the steps required to prepare and present a property tax appeal.

Now let's roll up our sleeves and get into some detail!

.

CHAPTER 2

How Property Taxes Are Levied

Before you prepare to make a property tax appeal, it is important that you understand how the property tax system works. You don't need to know every detail about the system, nor about how your local government functions, but you should have a general understanding so that you know how your taxes are set, what the monies are used for, and how the taxes are collected.

Let's take a look at a highly simplified example. Assume that we want to levy taxes in the mythical Village of Taxmania. Let's assume further that there are four properties in the village:

> 2 homes
> 1 store
> 1 church

To determine how much money they need to raise, the Taxmanian government officials will meet to establish an amount that they think will be sufficient to run their village during the next year. Then, they'll put together a budget for that amount that will pay for the costs of operating each department in their government. In this case, they estimate that they'll need $2,000 from real estate (property) taxes.

Their budget outlines how tax monies are to be spent, e.g., for schools, for any bonded indebtedness the Village has or anticipates, and for all other purposes. Then they set about raising the money (the $2,000) through taxation. Here is a summary of the steps they'll go through:

HOW PROPERTY TAXES ARE LEVIED

1. First, the Taxmanian Tax Assessor estimates the full market value of each taxable parcel. (In this example, assume the total appraised value for all taxable parcels adds up to $100,000.)

2. Next, the Assessor converts the appraised values into assessed values. In the state in which Taxmania is located, the law says that all taxable properties will be assessed at one-half of their appraised value. This is the assessment ratio.

(Appraised value) × (Assessment ratio) = (Assessed value)
   ($100,000)   ×   (0.50)   =   ($50,000)

3. Then, the Taxmanian Clerk (or Tax Collector) establishes a tax rate that will generate the tax revenues the town needs from the assessed property values.

(Tax to be collected) ÷ (All assessed values) = (Tax rate)
    ($2,000)   ÷   ($50,000)   =   (0.04)

4. Finally, the Clerk (or Tax Collector) prepares and mails the tax bills based on the tax rates and the assessed values for each piece of property. Note that the church property is exempt from property taxes.

	Home #1	Home #2	Store	Church	Totals
Appraised value:	$20,000	$30,000	$50,000	Exempt	$100,000
Assessment ratio:	×50%	×50%	×50%		×50%
Assessed value	$10,000	$15,000	$25,000		$50,000
Tax rate:	×0.04	×0.04	×0.04		×0.04
Tax bills:	$ 400	$ 600	$ 1,000		$ 2,000

THE ASSESSMENT PROCESS

Some comments may be in order to help you understand this process a bit better. In step one of the example, the Tax Assessor, or in some states, an independent appraiser, estimated the value of each taxable parcel. This value varies from one state to another. It is sometimes known as full value, true value, market value, appraisal value, just value, fair cash value, actual value, fair and reasonable market value, or full and fair value in money. Whatever the value is called, it represents, in concept at least, the value of the property in the current marketplace.

All assessments are based on full market value or a percentage thereof. Homeowners in jurisdictions where the assessment is based on full value will find it relatively easy to interpret their tax bills. More than half the states, however, require that local governments base the property tax on some fraction of market value. This can make it more difficult to understand your tax bill. In reading your tax bill, you may feel relieved to discover that the assessment on your $125,000 house is only $80,000. However, if your assessment is calculated with a 50-percent assessment rate, you are actually being taxed as though your home were worth $160,000 ($80,000 divided by 50%).

The frequency of appraisals for tax purposes also varies widely from one state to another. Because of the high cost of having appraisals done by independent appraisal firms, a full revaluation of a town, township, community, etc., may be done only once every ten years. In the Village of Taxmania, we assumed that it was done each year. In many states, however, a complete revaluation (reappraisal of all properties) within a taxing municipality (i.e., town, community, etc.) is done infrequently and is completed by an independent valuation firm.

The appraisal of new construction (versus existing construction), on the other hand, is done by the assessor instead of an independent appraisal firm. The assessment of property additions, known as an added assessment, is also done by the assessor. See Chapter 5, page 61, for a list of improvements that will and will not increase your tax assessment.

Looking back again at the first step on page 31, the assessor calculated the full value (market value) of all parcels in the Village of Taxmania ($100,000) by adding up the values established for each individual property. He added together the appraised values of the two homes ($20,000 and $30,000 respectively) and the store ($50,000). The church is tax-exempt.

ADJUSTING THE ASSESSMENT

In step two the *assessment ratio* is used to adjust the taxable values. Sometimes called the *tax multiplier*, this ratio will vary widely among states. It may be as low as 25 percent, or as high as 100 percent of the market value, or some percentage in between. Often, it is based on the cumulative value of properties sold during the tax year. It represents the relationship between assessed value and the current market value in the taxing municipality, as described earlier and defined by whatever term is used in your state. For example, if properties in the municipality are being assessed at one-half of their market value, the assessment ratio is 50 percent. To put it another way, the properties in the municipality are worth twice as much in the current market as the rate at which they are being assessed. Where a complete valuation is done every ten years, this ratio will normally decrease each year, if you assume a normal year-to-year rise in market values.

THE TAX RATE

In steps three and four, the clerk or the tax collector prepared the tax bills and mailed them out. Responsibility for this function will also vary among the states. (See page 35 for an example and explanation of a typical tax bill.)

The tax rate, mentioned in step three, may be stated as so many dollars per $100 or per $1,000 of assessed value, e.g., $2.05 per $1,000, or as millage (the tax rate expressed in mills, i.e., thousandths of a dollar).

As an additional example of how taxes are computed on a residence, let's use a *tax rate* of $0.75 per $100 of *assessed value,* and an *assessed value* of $50,000. We would calculate the taxes as follows: 50,000/100 = 500. This would give us the number of $100 units represented in the assessed value of $50,000. Next, we would multiply the number of $100 units (500 in this case) by $0.75 (500 × $0.75). The result would be $375. That is the amount of tax due that would appear on the homeowner's tax bill. If the homeowner has a mortgage, it is not uncommon for the mortgage company to require the payment of property taxes along with the mortgage payment. The mortgage company then forwards the amount due directly to the taxing municipality. This generally avoids any problems with late tax payments or nonpayment of taxes. In those cases where the homeowner owns his/her home free and clear, the homeowner is responsible for making these tax payments directly to the tax collector in his/her community.

Following is an example of a typical tax bill. To

understand properly what it means, I've included an
explanation of the more important parts of the bill.
Let's examine these at this time.

Term	Explanation
1990 Tax Bill	The top portion of the bill (the part above the phrase THIS IS NOT A TAX BILL—FOR ADVICE ONLY) is a summary of the taxes assessed for the current year. The bottom portion shows the estimated tax for the first and second quarters of the following tax year. These figures are estimated because the tax rate is not usually established until midyear in most states.
Block & Lot Number	These are numbers assigned to identify uniquely the property described in the tax bill. In some communities, the number used may be a permanent index number (P.I.N.) or the property may be identified by address only. See the tax map on page 87 for a visual example of a block and lot.
Add'l. Lot Numbers	Sometimes a property consists of more than one lot. In these cases, the additional lot numbers will be listed. These numbers should be checked by the homeowner to insure that the correct lots are being taxed.
Rate per $100	The rate established for use in calculating the amount of tax to be billed for each $100 of assessed

Term	Explanation
	value. To determine the "amount of tax" for any of the categories shown, simply multiply the "rate per $100" by the amount of the "total assessed valuation" (divided by $100), e.g., $181,500 (the total assessed valuation)/$100) = 1,815. Multiply 1,815 by any of the figures under "rate per 100," e.g., .434. The result ($787.70) is shown in the "amount of tax" column as the amount to be billed for the county tax.
Assessed Valuation— Land	The amount established by the tax assessor as the assessed value of the land. This may be set in several ways, such as so many do. per acre or part thereof, or of front footage and depth, etc. See Chapter 5 for further information.
Assessed Valuation— Improvements	The amount of assessed value for all taxable improvements on the land, e.g., buildings, barns, paved driveways, etc.

On the opposite page, you will find an example of a tax bill.

TAXATION OF PERSONAL PROPERTY

Our example did not include the taxation of personal property, such as furniture, etc. In some states, this type of property is included as a separate element

HOW PROPERTY TAXES ARE LEVIED

EXAMPLE OF TAX BILL

1990 FINAL TAX BILL			TOWNSHIP OF ANYTOWN		
Block Number	**Lot Number**	**Qual.**	**Description**	**Rate per $100**	**Amount of Tax**
1	70.4		County Tax	.434	787.70
			Dist. School Tax	1.077	1954.76
Property location:			Regional School Tax	.763	1384.85
143 Main Street			Local Tax	.476	863.94
			Total Tax	2.750	4991.25
Add'l. Lot Numbers:			Less Deduction		
None			for _____	____	____
			1990 Net Tax		4991.25
Account No.			Less 1990 Tax		
Bank Code		400S	Previously Billed		2486.55
Mort. Acct. No.			Balance of 1990 Tax		2504.70
Tax Bill No.					

1990 3rd Qtr. Due Aug. 1, 1990	1990 4th Qtr. Due Nov. 1, 1990	Assessed Valuation	
$1252.35	$1252.35	Land	57200
		Improvements	124300
Interest _____	Interest _____	Total	181500
Total _____	Total _____		

THIS IS NOT A TAX BILL—FOR ADVICE ONLY

1991 PRELIMINARY TAX BILL			TOWNSHIP OF ANYTOWN
Block No.	**Lot No.**	**Qual.**	**Explanation of Tax**
1	70.4		Preliminary Tax Is Equal To One Half (½) Of 1990 Total Net Tax
Property Location:			1991 Preliminary Tax Is:
Add'l Lot Numbers:			

1991 1st Qtr. Due Feb. 1, 1991	1991 2nd Qtr. Due May 1, 1991	2495.63
1247.82	1247.82	

of the assessment on your home. In any event, you should investigate the process in your state, ask questions of the assessor, and be sure that you understand and are aware of the approach used.

SUMMARY

By this time, you should have an adequate understanding of your property tax system. You should know why and how taxes are levied, how they are budgeted for, and how they are collected. Armed with this knowledge, you are now ready to learn about how the tax appeal process functions.

CHAPTER 3

.

How the Tax Appeal Process Works

Now that we've taken a look at the basic process of the property tax system, let's look at the legal basis for appealing your tax bill when you don't agree with the outcome. We'll begin with an explanation of the publication of the tax rolls.

Once a year, the assessor sets a value on each of the properties in the municipality and issues all the valuations in a complete tax roll that is announced, published, or posted for public review and/or grievance.

During this period of public announcement, the roll is usually considered tentative. This coincides with the grievance or appeal period in most states. After this grievance period, the roll becomes final and is turned over to the tax collector for collection. You should determine when this "tentative assessment" period occurs and consider having an informal discussion with your assessor about your tax bill before it comes to an end. If you can persuade the assessor to make an adjustment during this period, it will be easier for him to accomplish without interference from higher authorities (e.g., his supervisor, the county administrator, etc.). At this point, your approach can be informal and won't require a formal, written appeal. You can obtain the dates of this period of tentative assessment by calling your local tax assessor's office. In many states, this period occurs toward the end of the year. In any case, you should contact the assessor to find out when this period is before you begin gathering data and preparing your case. This way you will know just how much time you have to prepare.

A typical schedule of the major events during a tax year would be as follows:

Early January	Tax roll becomes final
April or May	Tax rates announced
June to August	Formal appeals accepted
September to October	Review board hearings
November	Results of hearings announced
December	Tentative tax rolls published

As previously mentioned, the above example is only typical and is not necessarily the schedule you need to follow. Check with your assessor or county administrator to confirm the exact tax calendar for your state.

Every state allows for some kind of local assessment review board. Most states will permit a second party who knows the facts of the case to file a grievance on the owner's behalf. Normally, this would be a tax consultant or an attorney.

In most states a written grievance or complaint is filed in accordance with state law and local regulations. This usually consists of a specific appeal form —perhaps one mandated by the state or one developed locally. The responsibility of finding out what form is to be used is up to the filer. Many grievance forms will require the property owner's signature to be witnessed by a notary public.

In most cases, you'll have to pay a nominal fee, probably between $5 and $25, to file an appeal. This fee may not be refundable, even if you win your case or withdraw your appeal for some reason.

Filing procedures will vary among states. The office of the municipality that made the assessment can tell you how and when to file a grievance. The time period between the opening of the tentative assessment roll and the deadline for filing a grievance usually is not more than ten to thirty days. In some states, the period for filing a grievance is as long as two and a half months and the publication of the tentative tax roll is many months earlier. *If the deadline is missed for filing a formal grievance, you must wait another year to file.*

Most states have a specific time of the year when an appeal may be filed, e.g., between June 1 and August 15. Likewise, the review board may hear cases only during a specific time of the year, e.g., September and October.

It is recommended that you do *not* mail the grievance statement because of the time used up in mailing or the possibility of its being lost. In some states you need not present your statement in advance but may bring it with you to the review board meeting. In every case, make sure to research the tax calendar in your area before you begin.

There are two types of grievances. One type concerns the decision of the assessor regarding an exemption (for example, a veteran, widow, senior citizen, etc.). This appeal or review process may not follow the same route as one concerning the assessment itself. In some states, the taxpayer would normally bring the omission of an exemption to the attention of the local assessor and it would be corrected. If there is a reason for not correcting it on the spot, an appeal would be necessary.

The other type of grievance concerns the assessment itself and will fall into one of these categories:

1. Illegal assessment
2. Unequal assessment

3. Errors in the assessment
4. Improper valuation of the property

All of these will be covered in detail in the chapters that follow.

You may want to have your case presented by an attorney or a property tax consultant. Both will be experienced in the procedures to follow, but both will charge you a fee. This fee is usually charged on a contingency basis; i.e., you pay only if a reduction in your taxes is achieved. Most review boards permit the homeowner to present his or her case without legal representation and will provide assistance for following the proper procedures.

CHAPTER 4

.

How Property Value Is Determined

HOW PROPERTY VALUE IS DEFINED

Before you begin gathering data to analyze what value should be set on your property, you need to understand how value is determined and why valuation is important and necessary. Let's examine some of the questions involved.

For any ad valorem tax (a tax law imposed at a rate or percent of a value), it is obviously important to start out with some concept and measure of value. This is because the property is to be taxed on the basis of that value.

We might then ask, "How is value to be determined?" Legislatures and courts have shown great creativity in defining what is to be used as a standard for measuring and comparing values among taxable properties in their jurisdictions. They use such terms as *cash value, actual cash value, true cash value, fair value,* and so forth.

Relatively few states or courts have actually established market value as the ultimate objective to be identified and measured. However, that is what appraisers and assessors, as well as attorneys and even judges, believe is to be measured, primarily because that is all that can be measured. Without measurability, there can be no basis for comparison, and therefore, no basis for equity. And equity, or "fairness," is one of the ultimate objectives of a property tax system, together with the notion that the value of one's property somehow indicates one's ability to pay taxes.

Therefore, the idea that value is identifiable and measurable has been combined with the search for equity (fairness) in the taxation of property. Thus, the concept of fair market value has emerged as one of the few, if not the only, appropriate methods for establishing taxable value.

In Chapter 4, we will examine the various approaches to property value. For now, let's look briefly at how property value is determined.

THE VALUE OF YOUR PROPERTY

Since an overvalued and overassessed property is one of the most common and most successful grounds for challenging your tax bill, it is extremely important to have a clear understanding of just how valuation works. Establishing the proper value for your property often is the key to your appeal. To win your case on the basis of establishing your property's value at a level lower than the one the assessor used, you must demonstrate that value using one of the recognized approaches to value. Therefore, it is vital for you to have a complete grasp on how to value your property. Let's learn more about how property value is established. But first, here is a highly condensed definition of each approach to value:

- Market approach—a comparison of the market value of your house to others of equal age, size, location, etc.
- Equity Analysis approach—a comparison of the assessed value of comparable properties.
- Cost approach—an estimate of the cost to acquire an acceptable substitute for a property with like utility.
- Income approach—an estimate of the earning power of a property (not used for nonincome producing properties).

For a residential property, you will be using either the market approach, the cost approach, or an equity analysis. Frequently, you will employ at least two of these methods together. Generally, the market approach is best because the truest test of value is the price for which a property can be sold in the marketplace. Thus, you should always start by using the market approach. Sales (market) data are available from real estate salespeople, appraisers, the tax assessor's office, and companies that specialize in supplying this type of information, e.g., REDI (Real Estate Data, Inc.).

In preparing your case, you should do both a market analysis and a cost analysis. Obtaining cost figures, however, may be more difficult because of the limited sources from which you can get them. An appraiser, the tax assessor, and real estate sales people will be the best sources. Sometimes libraries will carry this information also. The cost method is worth pursuing because it is the approach usually used by the tax assessor in compiling the data shown on your property record card in the assessor's office.

Some of the data for an equity analysis will be relatively easy to obtain. Each property in your tax district will have an assessed value shown in the tax records. These records are available to the public in the assessor's office. However, you will need square-footage information to complete this analysis. You may be able to secure it from the property cards, but the assessor may not let you see them. In that case, you will have to measure the properties yourself, or these measurements may be available from your market data. In addition, the equity approach is not recognized in every state. You can determine whether it applies to you by asking your assessor.

Now let's examine each of these methods in more detail.

The Market Approach

This method, which is sometimes called the comparative sales approach, is a comparison of the market value of your house to the market value of other homes of equal age, size, location, etc. Sometimes we refer to this as "obtaining comps." The market approach is, in general, the best approach to value and the one you should be using for your tax appeal.

The "market value" is defined as the highest price in terms of money that a property will bring in a competitive and open market under all conditions requisite to a fair sale, with the buyer and the seller each acting prudently and knowledgeably, and assuming the price is not affected by undue stimulus.

Implicit in this definition is the consummation of a sale as of a specified date and the passing of title from the seller to the buyer under conditions whereby:

1. Buyer and seller are typically motivated.
2. Both parties are well informed or well advised and each is acting in what he/she considers his/her own best interest.
3. A reasonable time is allowed for exposure in the open market.
4. Payment is made in cash or its equivalent.
5. Financing, if any, is on terms generally available in the community at the specified date and typical for the property type in its locale.
6. The price represents a normal consideration for the property sold unaffected by special financing amounts and/or terms, services, fees, costs, or credits incurred in the transaction.

Just think of this approach as an attempt to determine the market value (or whatever term your state uses) of a property—or the price that it would command in the marketplace—by comparing it to very similar properties. See pages 94–97 for an example of the market approach.

The Equity Analysis Approach

This approach compares the assessed values of similar properties on a square-footage basis. It can be used in the absence of current market data on comparable properties in your area, i.e., when there have not been any recent sales of residences like yours within a reasonable proximity of your home.

You may also use it as an additional example of why your assessment is too high. This method entails making an analysis of comparable homes on a square-footage basis and then making adjustments between the subject property (your home) and the comparable properties. You will be comparing items such as construction materials used, the types of extras installed in the home, the presence or absence of a paved driveway versus a stone driveway, etc. These adjustments are an attempt to allow for differences between the homes—and their assessed values—and allow for comparisons on a more equal basis. Dollar figures for adjustments may be obtained from valuation companies, state cost manuals, firms that supply such data, like Marshall & Swift Co., appraisers, tax assessors, and realtors. See pages 98–102 for examples of the equity approach. *When using this approach, all comparables must be within the same taxing municipality as your property.* The reason for this is that budgets, tax rates, revaluation dates, assessment ratios, etc., vary among taxing municipalities. There may be important differences between the way cities tax property that make comparisons between them useless. Finally, equity analysis may not be an acceptable approach in your state. Many states do allow this method. You should contact your assessor to see if this method is acceptable in your case.

The Cost Approach

The cost approach is used in valuing residential, industrial, commercial, and special-purpose properties, or when no market data are available. It is an estimate of the cost to acquire an acceptable substitute for a property with the same utility and similar improvements.

Standard costs for various construction elements, such as plumbing, electrical, heating, wall construction, etc., are used to "cost-out" the property. (To "cost-out" means to attach a cost or dollar value to each item for which you are being taxed, such as the cost of the plumbing required for a full bath, the cost of air-conditioning, or the cost of a garage or of a brick facing on an exterior wall.) To use the cost method, you will need *current* cost figures for your area from a valuation service, such as Marshall & Swift Co., or from your state tax office.

Because of the complexity of the method and the potential difficulty of obtaining current cost factors, you may find it extremely hard to use the cost approach for your residence. If you decide to use this method, if at all possible seek out help from an expert. The assessor, however, *will* use this method to value your property.

The Income Approach

There is one other approach to value, known as the income approach. This method won't apply to most people looking for property tax relief, but it's good to know about in case you run across it during your researches. Generally, it is used for income-producing properties, such as apartments or commercial office buildings. Income-producing property is typically purchased for investment purposes, and from the investor's point of view, earning power is the critical element that affects the property's value.

The income method uses the net income (gross income less operating expenses) derived from lease or rental payments divided by a capitalization rate developed for the type of property and local area in which the property is located. The objective is to determine or estimate the property's value by using these factors.

Again, this approach is more often used for properties other than what we are concerned with here. You will *not* be using it for a tax appeal on your residence.

SUMMARY

Keep in mind that the best approach to determine the value of your home is the market analysis. The data you'll need to put together a market-data-based appeal are readily available from many sources. Some suggested sources are realtors, appraisers, tax assessors, a company called REDI (Real Estate Data, Inc.) headquartered in Florida with representatives throughout the country—see your phone book.

The cost approach is most difficult to compile, and the sources for the cost figures you would need are limited. The tax assessor will usually have valued your property using this approach on the property record card. Don't be intimidated if you are unable to use this approach. Remember that your best approach is the market data analysis. The cost approach can serve as an additional justification for your case if you need it.

The equity approach is as easy to use as the market approach, but may not be a recognized method in your state. If it is, however, you'll compile the data using the same comparables as for your market approach.

CHAPTER 5

.

Adjustments to Value

With either the market data analysis or the equity analysis approach to value, it will be necessary to make adjustments between the comparable properties and the subject property (*your* property). The purpose of this is to equalize the properties for comparison purposes by compensating for any differences between them. For example, one of the comparable properties may have a garage or a fireplace while the subject (your property) does not. In this case, you'll have to adjust the value of the comparable property downward before you can use it as a valid comparison. Or the reverse may exist, if your property has a paved driveway and a comparable property does not. In this case, you'd have to adjust the value of the comparable property upward before you could use it as a valid comparison for your property.

Most of the adjustments involve physical factors. For examples of some of the more common adjustments, see the property record card examples in Chapter 7. The dollar figures used are obtained from cost manuals or from data supplied by firms such as Marshall & Swift. An appraiser, the tax assessor, or a Realtor can help you obtain the current figures.

The adjustments are always applied to the value of the comparable properties. They are never made to the value of the subject property. This technique changes the value of the comparable property so that when the values of the two properties are compared, it yields a better indication of relative value.

When the comparable property includes an adjustable element that is not shared by the subject property, the value of the comparable is adjusted downward. For example, let's say that the comparable property has a garage, and the subject property does not. The overall value of the comparable is adjusted by a preestablished amount that represents the value of a garage. The actual dollar amount is determined by periodic studies in similar geographic areas and is published in cost manuals produced by cost valuation firms. When the subject property contains an adjustable element that is not contained in the comparable property, the value of the comparable is adjusted upward. Thus, by adjusting the value of one home by the cost factor for the element, such as the garage, the two properties should become more equal in value. The differences between the two properties have been minimized, and by making the appropriate adjustments to value, the element is treated as if it did exist for both properties. The assumption is that the amount of the adjustment is the dollar difference that the presence or absence of the element (in this case, a garage) makes in the selling price or value of a house.

Adjustments typically are made for the following reasons:

1. *Time.*
Change continually affects the real estate market. During an inflationary period, the value of property tends to rise. In a deflationary period, the reverse is true. The best data for this adjustment is the price for which a property sold. For example, assume that a property sold three years ago for $80,000 and sold again today for $96,000. That would be an increase of 20 percent over three years or an average for each year of almost 7 percent. This adjustment for time

during this period of about 7 percent per year could also be applied to other comparable properties. By way of comparison, a comparable property that had sold two years ago would be valued by increasing the prior sales prices by 14 percent (7% × 2 years). If it sold for $85,000 two years ago, this kind of adjustment indicates that it would be worth about $96,900 today. You must be careful, however, to check that no other changes, such as physical improvements, have occurred to the property. If there have been changes, you must also make an adjustment for them.

2. *Location.*

Where the only significant difference between two properties is their relative locations, as reflected by a difference in sales price, an adjustment is made. For example, assume that a property with a better location than another sold for $80,000, while the property in the poorer location sold for $65,000. The adjustment for location, assuming all other elements were equal, would be to add 23 percent ($80,000/$65,000 = 123%, or a difference of 23%). If you were to use these two properties as comparables for your property, and the subject property (yours) has a location similar to the property having the better location, then the value of the poorly located property must be adjusted by adding 23 percent if it is to be used as a comparable.

3. *Physical condition.*

Where one property is in good condition and the other needs considerable maintenance, an adjustment may be made to compensate for the depreciation or physical deterioration. If two properties sold at about the same time, their locations were similar, and one was in good physical condition while the other needed considerable maintenance, you would use their sales prices to adjust for physical condition. For example, assume that the property in good condition sold for $80,000 and the other sold for $70,000. The difference would be 14 percent ($80,000/$70,000 = 114%, or a difference of 14%). Thus, you would make an adjustment of + 14 percent for depreciation to the property in poor condition. The new value would then be $79,800.

4. *Contributory value of a component.*

If there is a difference in the amenities contained in two properties, a dollar adjustment may be made. Items such as garages, fireplaces, paved driveways, etc., fall into this category. Assume that two houses sold at about the same time. One sold for $80,000 and had a garage, while the other sold for $76,000 without a garage. The contributory value of the garage then would be $4,000.

To illustrate the application of these adjustments, let's look at an example in tabular form. Table 1 shows the adjustable elements to be considered to arrive at a final value for the comparable properties and the subject property. Table 2 shows the lump-sum adjustments and the concluded value of each property in terms of adjusted sales price.

Adjustments will be required for time, the floor area, the basement, the garage, and lot size.

The adjustments are based on the following:

1. Time—advance in the market of 2 percent per year. The annual average inflation rate derived from government agencies or real estate associations.
2. Lot size—depths of 115 to 130 are typical ($200 less for 100 feet of depth and $200 more for 156

feet of depth). Contact an appraiser, tax assessor, or realtor for figures to use.

3. Floor area—$8.50 to $10.50 per square foot of value was used. Contact an appraiser, tax assessor, realtor, or construction company for average figures.
4. Basement—a value of $825 was used for a full basement. Derived from a cost manual—see assessor, appraiser, or realtor.
5. Garage—a value of $700 from market data was used. Contact a realtor, tax assessor, or appraiser for figures to use.

Based on the adjusted sale prices from Table 2, the value indicated for the subject property falls between $76,838 and $80,240. Since comparison #3 required the fewest adjustments, it is considered to be the strongest indicator of value. A value for the subject property of $76,800 ($76,838 rounded to the nearest one hundred) tends to be substantiated by the data available.

TABLE 1
COMPARATIVE SALES DATA

	Subject	Comp. #1	Comp. #2	Comp. #3
Sales price	—	$76,200	$76,800	$77,100
Date of sale	—	1/86	3/88	4/89
Age	10 yrs.	9 yrs.	9 yrs.	10 yrs.
Condition	Good	Good	Good	Good
Lot size (ft.)	50x127	50x117	50x156	50x115
Floor area (sq. ft.)	1923	1962	2008	1936
Full basement	No	Yes	Yes	Yes
Garage	2-car	None	None	None
Quality	Good	Good	Good	Good
Utilities	Avg.	Avg.	Avg.	Avg.
Site improvements	Avg.	Avg.	Avg.	Avg.
Location	Good	Good	Good	Good

TABLE 2
LUMP-SUM ADJUSTMENTS AND ADJUSTED PRICES
FOR COMPARABLE SALES

Adjustment	Subject	Comp. #1	Comp. #2	Comp. #3
Time	—	+ $4,575	+ $1,535	—
Lot size	—	—	− $200	—
Floor area	—	− $410	− $893	− $137
Basement	—	− $825	− $825	− $825
Garage	—	+ $700	+ $700	+ $700
Total Adjustment	—	+ $4,040	+ $317	− $262
Actual sale price	—	$76,200	$76,800	$77,100
Adjusted sale price	—	$80,240	$77,117	$76,838

THE EFFECT OF HOME IMPROVEMENTS

The first list below shows improvements and changes to your property that do not require adjustments and generally do not add to your assessed value (except, as noted, if they contribute to a major improvement in the overall physical condition of the property). The second list shows elements that *can* affect your assessed value and are considered by the assessor when valuing a property for assessment purposes.

Home Improvements That May Not Increase Your Assessment

Inside the Home
New furnace
Hot-water heater
Plaster repairs
Painting, wallpapering
Small closets or
  built-ins
New ceilings
Interior surfacing
Replace wiring
Plumbing fixtures

Outside the Home
Repairing masonry
New roof
New porch, steps, stairs
Repair fire escape
New window sashes &
  sills
Insulation
Weather-stripping
Awnings & window
  shutters

Inside the Home
Light fixtures
New floor surfacing
Leveling a floor
Addition to vents
Remodeling fireplace
New fire exits
New cabinets &
   countertops
Ventilating fan
New sink
Foundation repairs

Outside the Home
New gutters &
   downspouts
Outside painting
Repairing dry rot
Decorative screens
Street trees
Replacing sidewalks
Outdoor cable & lights
Repairing walks
Replacing sheds &
   garages
New fences or walls
Addition of retaining
   wall
Lawns & lawn
   sprinklers
Replacing garage doors

Note: It should be emphasized that a combination of these improvements could result in a considerable increase in the market value of your property. The physical condition of your property may also have to be adjusted for as indicated earlier in this chapter.

Elements That Could Affect Your Assessment

Structure (framing and foundation)
Overall quality of the property
Construction (frame, brick, stone, etc.)
Roof (type, slope, presence or absence of gutters/eaves
Wiring and fixtures (type and grade)
Heating and air-conditioning (type and size)
Detail of finish used in rooms (floors, walkways, trim)
Detail in bathrooms (quantity, type, and grade)
Plumbing (type and grade)
Exterior finish

Windows (storm windows, screens, and type)
Age (the year built, the remaining economic life, effective age)
Square footage

Note: All of these elements must be viewed with respect to their functional utility or usefulness and desirability in the marketplace. Poor design, inadequate lighting, cooling, or heating, and rooms that are too small to be functional should be considered as to their impact on utility.

ADJUSTMENTS FOR LAND VALUE

One of the more significant adjustments to be made is for the value of the land on which improvements (e.g., a house or a building) are located. For example, in the case where one of the comparables you are using is on five acres of land and your home is on three acres. In this case, an adjustment is necessary for the difference in the amount of land.

Since it is often necessary to analyze differences in size and shape of comparable properties to apply uniform methods of valuation, let's talk a little more about land valuation.

There are five ways in which to compare land values. You should follow the method used by the assessor on the property record card. Similarly, in making adjustments, use the same method selected by the assessor for your property and the comparables.

The five methods are:

1. *Front foot.*
This method is based upon the proposition that frontage significantly contributes to value. A front foot is a strip of land that is one foot wide, that fronts on a property and continues to the rear of the parcel

(a measure across the front of a property, e.g., from right to left from one side to the other. This distance often is measured in terms of a standard depth and its value is determined using standard-depth tables (found in real estate reference books in libraries or available through appraisers or tax assessors using this approach). A depth table is a guide used to determine changes in land value caused by variation in the depth of lots where the land is bought on the basis of a front-foot. The front foot method is most often used in valuing commercial and industrial property, but can be used for residential properties also.

2. *Square foot.*

This method is used for irregularly shaped land where frontage is not a dominant factor. It is expressed in dollars per square foot. If, for example, a parcel contained 10,000 square feet and the value of comparable properties of similar size in your area was $1.00 per square foot, the value of the land would be $10,000.

3. *Acre and section.*

An acre contains 43,560 square feet and a section consists of 640 acres. Obviously then, this method would be used for the valuation of larger properties, such as shopping centers, industrial parks, ranch and farm properties, etc.

4. *Site.*

This method is used when the market does not indicate a significant difference in lot value although there may be a significant difference in lot size. It is used in cluster developments, planned unit developments, and industrial sites.

5. *Units buildable.*

This method is used for apartment buildings,

parking garages, and other properties where the unit of comparison is the selling price per unit.

Some assessors employ other arbitrary methods in taxing municipalities where the residences are on one or more acres. They assign an arbitrary value to the first acre, another to the second acre, and a smaller value to any acreage above that. As long as the method is standard within the municipality and is uniformly applied therein, the tax basis can be considered fair. Market values, however, can tend to distort the fairness of methods like this one.

SUMMARY

Improper valuation of property, whether it be the land or the improvements, is the key or crux to most tax appeals. You should, therefore, spend as much of your time as possible on gathering data to support the value you establish for your property. It is important that you properly and adequately show its value. Reread this chapter to make sure that you understand valuation. It might also help to go to your local library to obtain a good book or two on this subject. See References, page 147, e.g., *Property Assessment Valuation, Fundamentals of Real Estate Appraisal, How to Appraise Your Own Home,* and *Appraising the Single Family Residence.*

.

CHAPTER 6

Other Reasons To Challenge Your Property Tax

In Chapter 1, step two, we looked at the criteria on which we could base an appeal. In Chapter 4, we discussed the various approaches to value covered in step two. Now we will examine in more detail the other criteria, such as what types of illegal and unequal assessments there are, what kind of record errors we might encounter, and any other situations we ought to examine. Let's look at some other reasons to appeal your property tax.

ILLEGAL ASSESSMENTS

An illegal assessment is one that should not have been made at all, or not in the manner in which it was made.

Perhaps part of the assessed property is supposed to be excluded from the property tax because of the type of property it is. Examples of this are properties or portions thereof that are used by charitable, religious, or benevolent organizations or nonprofit associations. Perhaps part is to be exempted because of its ownership or use. If you are unsure as to whether this applies to you, you can look up the possible exclusions or exemptions in the tax administration handbook for your state. A copy should be available at your tax assessor's office. You could also check with the local authorities in your area, such as the tax collector, tax assessor, county tax administrator, etc.

Here are some specific areas in which you can look for an illegal assessment:

OTHER REASONS TO CHALLENGE YOUR PROPERTY TAX

1. Property is assessed at more than the legal percentage. For example, the limit is 50 percent of market value and the property is assessed at 75 percent of market value. Ask your tax assessor how properties should be valued in your area, such as at full market value or a legally mandated percentage thereof as found in your state or local property tax laws.

2. Improper classification of property. All properties are assessed within their own class, such as residential, commercial, industrial, farmland, etc. Check to see if your property is properly classified as residential, and if there are subcategories within residential, whether or not your property is classified under the right one. For example, there may be subcategories 1–10 under residential where category 9 may be houses that are 2,000 to 2,500 square feet and category 10 includes those larger than that. Yours may be category 10 when it belongs in category 9. In the tax administration handbook (used by the tax assessor) there may be pictures of houses that fall within each category. Yours may not even come close to the pictures shown for the category in which you have been assessed. If appropriate, check whether reclassification would lower your taxes.

3. Assessment higher than state-issued sales-assessment ratio. This is a ratio, calculated by the state tax authorities, based on the market values within each taxing district, that is announced each year and is available from your local assessor or county tax office. It represents the average at which properties compare to the market value in an area. Sometimes the review board will not change an assessed value when the value you establish does not fall outside a certain percentage of the ratio, e.g., plus or minus 15 percent. On the other hand, when you

prove a lower value for your property, the local tax assessor may make the change for you despite the existence of this guideline. Check with your assessor as to whether or not the ratio is used in your state, and if so, what it is in your tax district. Some states do not use the sales-ratio approach because market values for properties are established each year. In others, revaluations occur infrequently and sales within the tax year are used to establish average values, such as with the sales-ratio approach.

4. Assessor used wrong approach in valuation according to state manual. For example, the manual may require the market approach and the cost approach was used.

5. Some states require an assessor to inspect a property before raising the assessment. This may or may not be indicated on the property record card. If it isn't, ask your assessor whether or not the property was inspected. If you can prove that there was no inspection (and that may be difficult) you have a small point to argue about. It may be impossible to get a tax reduction based solely on this condition.

6. No notice of increased assessment was issued or received. The assessor is required to notify you of this by direct mail or by public notice. Check to see whether it was done.

PERSONAL EXEMPTIONS

Exemptions are granted for a variety of reasons to individuals who own property. These are established by law in each state. They are applied against the tax you owe and provide a small tax reduction if you are entitled to them. For example, in some states, the exemption for a veteran is $50 per year. This isn't substantial, but every bit of tax relief helps. A list of typical personal exemptions for which you may qualify appears below. Keep in mind that the items on the list do not apply in all states because laws vary from state to state.

Typical Personal Exemptions

1. Veterans
2. Hardship cases (low income)
3. Disabled veterans
4. Rehabilitated property
5. Disabled veterans who live in "specially adapted" housing
6. Persons owning mortgaged property
7. Widows of veterans
8. Fire equipment
9. Blind
10. Certain agricultural land
11. Elderly
12. Most tangible personal property
13. Reforestation
14. Property of Red Cross
15. Persons 65 years of age and over
16. Equipment to prevent air and water pollution
17. Tax sale
18. Personal property of railroads
19. All growing crops (farmland)
20. Intangible personal property

Note: Not all of these exemptions apply to residential property, and some will not apply in your state, but most of them do. Check with your tax assessor for a list of those that apply in your area.

VALUATION GUIDELINES

The assessor must follow an official manual. Many assessors follow an official valuation manual issued by a state agency, or at least they are supposed to unless they have a valid reason to depart from it. The manuals can be purchased or referenced at a county library. You can buy these manuals at minimal cost, or possibly your assessor will allow you to examine them while you are in his or her office. However, they can be rather confusing and full of detail and terminology that is not readily understood by the average, nonexpert taxpayer.

Should you hire an expert to help you with your case or to interpret these manuals? Property owners do challenge assessments successfully—without help from experts. However, you may want to consider having an expert, a tax attorney or property tax consultant, review your documentation before you present your appeal. He or she may be able to point out something that you have overlooked or make suggestions about your materials. The cost should be minimal, and you may feel more confident having had some support or constructive criticism. After gathering your data, you may decide to have an expert handle the negotiations with the assessor or review board. There are many ways to handle your appeal. You have to decide how you will be most comfortable and what approach will be most cost effective and successful for you.

Others, including lawyers, developers, and large corporations with considerable expertise, prefer to have some help from specialists. Some have specialists check out every real estate tax bill and change in assessed value.

Independent experts have several advantages.

The most important of these is expert knowledge of recent sales, rentals, and market trends, knowledge of the procedures the assessor should be using, and knowledge of what the review boards have been doing in similar cases.

There are various ways in which the consultant may charge the client. The consultant may charge by the hour or by the day. Then the fee is not contingent upon the outcome of the work. A common arrangement is a flat fee for a preliminary review of an assessment. The specialist reports to the client on the fairness of the assessment and on any grounds for reduction. Then, if the client is interested in retaining the specialist for further work, the two may agree on an additional fee. In most sizable cities, there are firms that can be retained to get real estate taxes reduced for a percentage of the savings. The contingent-fee arrangements vary. The principal appeal of this kind of an arrangement is that you pay only for results.

UNEQUAL ASSESSMENTS

An unequal assessment is one made at a higher proportion of full value than the average of the other parcels on the roll. It can fall into one of three categories:

1. Property assessed at more than market value. For example, you can show that the market value of your house is $100,000, but the assessed value set by the tax assessor is $120,000.
2. Assessments on similar properties are lower. This is an example of the equity approach to value. Here, you have found comparable prop-

erties within your neighborhood that are assessed lower than your property.

3. Property recently purchased for less than assessed value. In this case, the assessed value may be $100,000, but the property, either yours or a comparable one, was sold recently for $80,000.

These categories show you the *causes* for an unequal assessment. You then can use, for example, the market *approach to value* to demonstrate that the value of your property is different (hopefully lower) than the value of comparable properties. An *approach to value* helps you prove your case by comparison, whereas a *cause* for unequal assessment helps you identify the condition that exists.

Politicians can try to trick the public by setting assessments below market value. If your assessment is lowered, then the tax rate must be increased in order to collect the necessary amount of tax revenue. The same amount of tax is collected, but the taxpayers are fooled into thinking they've gotten a break.

An important test for fairness of your assessment is not just its relationship to market value. It is also whether or not it is fair in relation to assessments on other properties in your area. For example, if you have land that is worth $800 per acre, but it is assessed at $600 per acre, you may think you are getting off cheaply. However, if nearby land comparable to yours is assessed at only $200 per acre, you are paying three times as much real estate tax as you should.

MECHANICAL ERRORS

Many times you'll find miscalculations, clerical errors, and plain mistakes in the tax records that are used to determine your tax bill. As discussed earlier, you will be checking for these types of situations when you inspect your property record card and other records used at the tax assessor's office. Here are some of the things you should do to check these records.

Even if you don't agree with some of the cost factors or depreciation percentages or don't understand them, check the computations for mistakes.

Finding a mistake in a building size or in simple computations (and there seem to be lots of mistakes) can put you in line for a sizable reduction.

It is estimated that 5–10 percent of all parcels are erroneously inventoried or do not appear on the current assessment rolls at all. Many municipalities have no system to advise assessors of buildings that have been burned, demolished, or otherwise removed. If you are being taxed, for example, for a detached garage that no longer exists, you will want to appeal.

Here are some other types of things that you can check:

1. The dimensions of your land are wrong. You may own one and a half acres, but are being taxed on two acres because the dimensions on your record card are incorrect or you have land that measures 100′ by 70′ and the record shows it as 120′ by 70′.

2. The dimensions of buildings or improvements are wrong. If, for example, you owned a rectangular building, but the length on one side was shown as being twenty feet and the length of the opposite side was shown as twenty-five feet.

3. The descriptions of buildings are wrong. Perhaps the record showed your house as having a brick face on one side, when it was frame.

4. The description of your land is wrong. Perhaps the description includes part of your neighbor's land and you are being taxed for it.

5. The wrong property assessed. Here the lot and block numbers may be incorrect, or the property you are being taxed on is not yours.

6. Arithmetic errors. Check all computations, whether or not you understand where the factors used were derived from.

7. Failure to note depreciating on-site conditions. Part of your property may be unusable; e.g., it may contain huge gullies. Or something on your property may be affecting its value; e.g., quicksand or sulphur odors.

8. Failure to note depreciating off-site influences. For example, there may be something on property adjoining yours that materially affects the value of your property—not an unsightly house, but perhaps a factory producing toxic fumes that drift onto your property.

9. The grade and quality of improvements are wrong. Maybe you put stones on your driveway and you are being taxed for a paved driveway.

10. Important information has been omitted from the record card. For example, the card doesn't show a calculation for depreciation. As a result, your property is overassessed.

11. The record is out-of-date. Perhaps your record card hasn't been updated for ten years. There may have been many changes that could lower your assessed value. For example, you haven't done any maintenance and your property is in poor physical condition, but the records show that it is in good condition.

12. Finished areas are listed incorrectly. Perhaps your record card indicates that your basement is completely paneled, has an acoustical ceiling, and hardwood floors, when in fact it is unfinished.

13. Property assessed in the wrong class. For ex-

ample, residential property is wrongly classified as commercial.

14. Property listed in wrong assessment district. This is rare, but it happens. Perhaps you are being taxed by a district with high taxes, when your property is located within the next tax district where the taxes are much lower.

15. Personal property included in your assessment, when it is excluded in your state. Most states do not tax personal property, or did tax it many years ago, but don't now. Your property may still be shown on the record. If it is, you are being taxed for it.

16. Maintenance items used to increase assessments. Unless there are many items that, when combined, increase the value of your house, your assessment should not be increased for routine maintenance. Look for these on your record card and compare them to the list in Chapter 5.

17. Income valuation approach used in error. State laws usually specify the method to be used to assess properties. See your state manual. Usually, the cost approach is used to value residential properties.

18. Standard cost manual improperly used. For this you will need access to the cost manual used by assessors in your district. You will have to cross-check all the factors selected by the assessor from the manual to arrive at the costs shown on your record card.

19. Depreciation allowances made in error. If the depreciation used on your property is significantly different from your comparables, you can challenge it. For example, your house has been depreciated 10 percent when the comparables have been depreciated 20 percent. Keep in mind, though, that this allowance is based on the condition of your house and of the comparables.

20. Highest and best use listed incorrectly. You probably won't be able to use this for your residence. If you're interested, see one of the additional readings in Appendix C.

21. Assessment higher than construction cost. If you can prove that your house, which was constructed very recently, cost much less to build than the assessor's cost analysis shows, you can get a tax reduction. This assumes that the assessor used a current, approved cost manual.

22. Shoddy construction. For example, you are assessed for average-or-better construction when yours is signficantly below standard.

23. Lack of utilities. Access to electricity, water, etc., isn't available on your property, but you are being taxed about the same as comparable properties that have access to utilities.

24. Exemptions for property use. For example, the property may be used for military purposes, or a portion of the property is leased to an organization composed entirely of veterans, or the land has been dedicated for cemetery purposes and is used by a nonprofit cemetery company, or the property is designated for nonprofit use such as in part or totally by a charitable, religious or benevolent organization, or part or all of the property is designated as a historic site.

25. Environmental restrictions. Perhaps part of your property is unusable because of environmental laws or regulations. Check to see whether these restrictions—which lower the value of your property—are recorded properly on your record card.

26. Exemptions, such as veteran or homestead. See the list earlier in this chapter for possible exemptions that may be available in your area. Check with your assessor to verify which ones are used in your area.

27. Easement restrictions not considered. Perhaps there is an easement (someone has a written, legal right to use a portion of your property for access to another property) that materially affects the value of your property versus comparable property in your neighborhood. The assessor may not have taken this into account when valuing your property.

28. The age of the building is listed incorrectly. For example, your house was built in 1982, but the tax record shows that it was built in 1987.

29. The number of stories is wrong. For example, the assessor counts a partly finished basement as a story.

30. The overall description is incorrect. For example, your home is described as a three-family type when actually it is a two-family.

SUMMARY

Now that we've reviewed the various reasons for which a property may be unfairly taxed, be certain that, when you discover them relative to your property, you list them on a separate sheet of paper. This will assure that you don't overlook any of them and that you can systematically review each of them with the assessor.

·

CHAPTER 7

Researching Your Tax Appeal

Now we're going to put all the information you've been learning to good use. There's plenty of research for you to do. When doing it, remember that you will be searching for data to support a lower assessed value for your property, and that the best way to accomplish that is to gather market data. You'll also be looking for illegal and unequal assessments, and errors in your tax records. Details are important here, so take your time and check for all the possible ways to get your assessment reduced.

To properly research your tax appeal, you should follow the procedures outlined below.

1. *Identify comparable properties and gather information about them.*

The first step is to drive around your neighborhood in search of any properties that are like yours in terms of age, size, design, and construction. Make notes about their addresses or relative locations so you can locate them on the tax maps and in the tax records when you visit the tax assessor's office. Later on, you will also want to determine if they were sold recently, and gather information about the assessments on their land and improvements.

A comparable property is one that is similar in location, age, design, size, and construction to your own residence.

A comparable may be identified by locating it physically on the ground by its relative location to your residence or other landmarks in the area.

It is most important to identify a comparable that is located in the same general area as your own residence. If your home is in one area and the comparables you select are in an area far away across town, your chance of winning your case is minimal.

Likewise, it is important to select a comparable of similar age to your own residence. The depreciation factor on a twenty-five-year-old house will be significantly different from that on a five-year-old house.

Next in importance is design. Comparing two colonial houses is much more convincing than comparing a colonial to an ultramodern home.

Size differences are of lesser importance provided that the difference between comparables is not significant. You can always compensate for minor differences by comparing them on a square-footage basis.

Construction-material differences can also be compensated for, as you will see later.

Be sure to identify at least six comparable properties, so that later you can select the three that best make your case. Record the information about each comparable on separate sheets. Blank forms have been provided for your use at the end of the book. Later in this chapter, we'll work our way through a few examples that will help you fill out these forms. As you gather more data about each property, continue to keep all of the information about one property together on the same sheet of paper.

Now you are ready for a visit to your local assessor's office. Depending on the organization in your state, your property taxes may be administered from a county office or a local office within your municipality. Check the government pages in your phone book for the telephone number and address of the proper office. Call them for directions and information on where your property record card and other related information may be located. The object of this visit is to familiarize yourself with the information that is available to you, collect data about your comparables, and review your property record card (the assessor's worksheet that is used to determine the assessed value of your property).

You will want to request a copy of this card so that you can closely examine it in the privacy of your own home or office. When you do this, you will be looking for record errors or anything else upon which to base your appeal.

While you are at the assessor's office, you should also examine the tax list and the tax maps. From the tax list you will be able to identify your property and the comparable properties by lot and block number, by street address, or by a permanent index number (if your state uses a parcel identification system to tie together ownership, tax maps, and tax-roll entries).

2. Identify your comparables on the tax list.

The tax list is a public record and can be found in the local assessor's office or at the county tax office. It is filed by year and shows all properties within the municipality by owner's name, in alphabetical order, and by lot and block number in numerical order. You may find books for several tax years on display.

Be very careful when comparing the results of your ground search with the tax records. There may be two or more properties that look alike or have the same owner.

Copy all the information about your comparables that you find on the tax list onto a sheet of paper for later use. (You may find it easier to record it directly on the blank market-analysis forms.) This information should include lot and block number, property address, property class, owner's name, the assessed value of the land, improvements, and the total, and if given, the size of the land.

3. *Locate your comparables on the tax maps.*

Tax maps for your municipality can be found in the local assessor's office or, for all municipalities in the county, at the county tax office. They may also be accessible in the county clerk's office.

The tax maps will give you the dimensions of your land and of the comparables. They will also help you to identify properly the comparables.

There may be as many as twenty or thirty maps for a larger municipality, and they may be grouped together in several binders. The maps consist of a set of index maps (see page 86) and a set of tax maps (see page 87). The top maps, sometimes as many as four or five of them in a larger municipality, are called index maps. They will help you to identify the specific tax map that contains the particular lot and block for which you are looking. The index map is a representation of a larger area of the municipality than the maps on which the blocks and lot numbers are found.

The circled numbers (they are sometimes enclosed within a square) on the index map refer to the tax map on which the lot and block can be found. The tax map page number usually is located in the upper right corner of each tax map. (Always ask if you aren't certain or if the markings aren't clear.)

When you have positively identified the particular parcel you are looking for, record the dimensions and shape of the parcel on a sheet of paper for later use. *Never trust the dimensions shown on a tax map in the assessor's office.* Always obtain a map of survey for your property. When you purchased your property, one of the many papers you received from your attor-

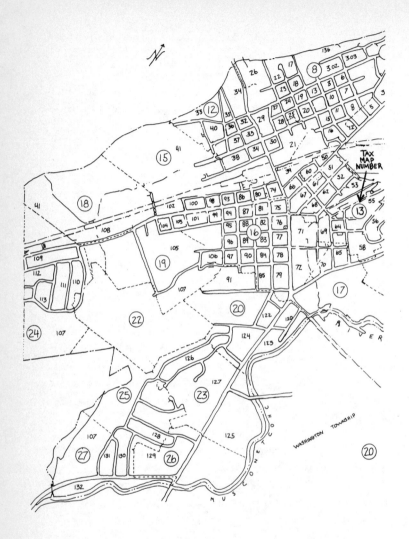

Index Map

Tax Map

ney or the title company was a map of survey. It shows the location of your property by use of a ground map. It will indicate the dimensions of your land, the relative location of any improvements thereon, such as your house, and will indicate the lot and block number or other identification of your property. You should have a copy with your closing papers or a copy can be obtained from your closing attorney or the title or escrow company that handled your closing.

4. *Obtain a copy of your property record card from the assessor's office.* (See pages 90 and 91).

This record contains all of the information that the assessor has used to value your property for tax purposes. It may not be totally accurate, but in some cases, that will be to your advantage. In some states, these cards are not considered public records. Therefore, the assessor is not required to supply you with copies of the cards for the comparable properties that you have identified.

Likewise, in these states, the assessor is not required to furnish you with a copy of your own property record card until about a week to ten days prior to when your appeal is heard. This means that you will have less time to prepare the information for your appeal.

You may have to copy all of the information that you need onto a sheet of paper. The items you need are the building dimensions, all items being assessed and their assessed values, building age, type of construction, depreciation, land size, any changes in assessed values for any reason, and the computations used for all assessments.

Ask the assessor how the land is assessed and note the answer. Compare it to the method used on your property record card.

If the record card shows data for front depth, standard depth, etc., the front-foot method was used. If square footage data are shown, the square foot method probably was used.

See Chapter 5 under "Adjustments for Land Value" for a further explanation.

Most assessors will furnish the property owner with a copy of his or her property record card upon request. Also ask for the property record cards for the comparables you will be using. If the assessor won't give them to you, ask him or her to give you the total assessed square footage and the year of construction for each of the comparables that you have researched.

He/she may or may not be willing to supply this information. If not, you will have to visit the building department, the engineer's office, or the planning department, where again, you'll have to solicit the cooperation of the staff to obtain the needed information. Usually these offices are located within the same building or in close proximity to the assessor's office. Often, they will bring out architectural drawings and help you to secure the needed information from them.

If you cannot acquire the data there, you may have to physically measure the comparable houses and/or ask the owners if they can supply the data. This may require a bit of diplomacy, but in most cases you will not have to resort to this kind of research.

5. *Obtain sales information about your comparables.*

You will also want to review the sales records for properties that have sold within the past one or two years in your neighborhood. These can also be found in the tax office, or they may be centralized at the county level in the county tax office. The sales infor-

PROPERTY RECORD CARD

FOLDER

CARD **164** OF   LOT **12-4**

ADDRESS

	OWNER OF RECORD		CODE NO		CLASSIFICATION **2 5F**				

BLOCK 164   LOC MAIN ST   LOT SIZE 3.6050
LOT 12-4   CLAS 25F

LAND $19,200 IMPROV. $55,900 TOTAL $75,100 DED. V1 02

DOE, JOHN & MARY
14 MAIN ST
TOWER, NJ   12345

	DATE OF SALE	SALES PRICE	MAP	BUILDING	EXMT CODE	TOTAL	YEAR	ADDED ASSESS.
	10-20-78	33,000 (1)		124,300	—	181,500	1983	
	2-9-79	131,845						
	8-24-80	166,000						
	1-14-86	140,000						

	LAND	%
	57,200	

PHOTO

LAND VALUATION DATA

Influence Factors:

FF	SF	AC	ST	Zone	Front	Depth	Back Lot Set Back	Standard Depth	Acre	Square Feet	Unit Value	Infl 1	Infl 2	Infl 3	Infl 4	Infl 5	Infl 6	Adjustment	Total Value
✓		✓		R-2					2.0										50,000
									1.0										5,000
									.605		2,500								1,500
				33							2.0								700

Total Land Value   **57,200**

1 = Depth   2 = Frontage   3 = Back Lot   4 = Triangular (30 or 60)   5 = Corner Lot   6 = Topography

SITE DATA

NEIGHBORHOOD
Rural	
Crossroads	Commercial
Suburban	Industrial
Urban	Mixed

Subdivision

INFLUENCES
Corner Lot	
Adjoining Alley	
Back Lot	
Street Light	
Sidewalks	
Underground Utilities	✓

SEWER
None	Private
Septic	Public ✓

WATER
None	Private
Well	Public

OTHER UTILITIES
Gas	Electric ✓

PROXIMITY TO SERVICES
Typical	Superior ✓
	Inferior

ROAD TYPE
None	
Dirt	✓
Gravel	
Paved	

TRAFFIC
Light	✓
Heavy	

Cul-de-Sac ✓
Extensive Easements

NEIGHBORHD CONFORMITY
Superior	Interior

NEIGHBORHOOD TREND
Stable	Improving
	Declining

TOPOGRAPHY
Level	High
Rolling	Low ✓

LANDSCAPING
Typical	Superior ✓
Detrimental View	Inferior
Enhancing View ✓	

NO. OF APTS
Type

SUMP PUMP
Yes	No
CONNECTED TO SEWER	
Yes	No

BUILDING PERMITS

APPEAL DECISION

C or S	LAND	BUILDING	TOTAL

NOTES

OCCUPANT

DATE

Left panel (construction details)

1	ROOF TYPE/ MATERIAL		5	FLOOR CONST/ FINISH		9	BUILT-INS	No	Dual	Cost
Flat	✓		Frame	Steel			Free-Standing Range			
Gable	✓		Conc. Slab	Other			Kitchen Facility			
Gambrel			Carpet	Wood			Drop-In Range	✓		
Shed			Ln./Vinyl	Other			Built-In Range Oven	✓		
Shingle		6	HEATING/ COOLING				Electric Oven			
Slate							Range Hood w. Fan	✓		
Copper			Electric	Coal			Dishwasher	✓		
Tile		2	FOUNDATION				Garbage Disposal			
Metal			Gas	None			Dishwasher			
Wood			Oil	✓	Other		Central Vacuum			
Pitched							Elec. Gar Dr Open			

2	FOUNDATION		10	FIREPLACES	No	Dual	Cost
Crawl Space	✓		1 Story Fireplace			
Conc. Slab			1½ Story Fireplace			
Conc. Blk			2 Story Fireplace	✓		1600
Post/Pier			Total			1600

3	BASEMENT		11	FINISHED ATTIC		
Basement Quality	17	GOOD		Per Cent of Attic Finish		
Area of Bsmt Finish				Quality of Attic Finish		

4	EXTERIOR WALLS				No	Dual	Cost
Siding	✓		4 Fixture Bath				
Brick			3 Fixture Bath	2	855		
Stone			2 Fixture Bath		625		
Aluminum	✓		Single Fixture				
Other (specify)			Kitchen Sink	1			
			Laundry Tub				
			Water Heater	½	2		
NOTES			Total	2	14480		

7	PLUMBING	No	Dual	Cost
Heating Quality	GOOD			
Heat Duct	✓	Own Duct	✓	6000
Air Conditioning Quality	GOOD			

NOTES

CARRIER CENTRAL AIR — 1 2 ST. CHIMNEY
WOOD DECK 12 × 24
CONC. TER. 36
BLT IN PORCH 3 × 6

Building Sketch / Floor Area Computations

FLOOR AREA COMPUTATIONS

Segment	Width × Length	Basement	First Story	Second Story	Third Story	Half Story
A-2Q	27 × 24-18	648	630	648		
B-2Q	14 × 12	168	168	168		
C-1	14 × 2	28	28			
D-2Q	14 × 22	308	308	308		
E1	10 × 19		190			
Total Floor Area		1124	1324	1124		

PORCHES/DECKS, GARAGES, CARPORTS, ETC.

Item	Width × Length	Area	Unit Cost	Cost	Conv. Fa	Dual Fa	Rept Cost	% Resid	Appraised Value
P-1	10 × 3	30	6.52		1.13		3555	1.1	
B.I.P	3 × 6	18							

COST CALCULATION

ITEM	AREA	RATE	BR ST	COST	REVISED
First Floor	1324	28.81		38,277	
Second Floor	1124	17.86		20,075	
Third Floor					
Half Story			TOTAL		
ROWHOUSE AND END UNIT FACTOR					
ADJUSTED BASE COST					

ITEM	AREA	RATE	DUAL	COST	
3 Basement	1124	1.35		5534	
Bsmt Finish			1		
4 Part Ext Wall					
5 Floor Slab Adj					
6 Heating	2448	.93	115	2065	
Cooling	2448	.57	115	1605	
7 Plumbing	2	1480.15		1700	
8 Built-Ins	1	440.1		440	
9 Built-Ins					
10 Fireplaces	1	16.00	130	2080	
11 Finished Attic					
WD DECK	288	2.67	130	768	
Unfinished Area					
Built-In Garage					
Bsmt Garage					
Open Porch	48	9.35	130	449	
Enclosed Porch					
CON. TER	36	3.80	1	137	
TOTAL BASE COST NEW				73,122	
COST CONVERSION FACTOR		1.71			
REPLACEMENT COST				125,039	
a depreciation					
b physical condition					
c 1.00 − (a + b)					
d 1.00 − economic obsolescence					
e 1.00 − functional obsolescence					
f 1.00 − other					
g (d × e × f)					
h (c × g) net residual				95	
h = replacement cost					

SUMMARY OF APPRAISAL

PRINCIPAL BUILDINGS		118,800
ACCESSORY BUILDINGS		5,500
TOTAL OF BUILDINGS		124,300
LAND VALUE		57,200
APPRAISED VALUE		

DESCRIPTIONS, REPLACEMENT COST, AND APPRAISAL OF ACCESSORY BUILDINGS

Building Identity	Class	Width	Depth	Floor	Roof	Yr. Blt	Walls	Area	Unit Cost	Cost	Conv Fa	Dual Fa	Rept Cost	% Resid	Appraised Value
ATT. GAR.		22	22					484	1.13		1.1	6079	90	5500	

STRUCTURAL AND ACCESSORY ADDS

VERBAL − ASK TO RETURN EVENINGS

			TOTAL	5500

Enumerator E.P.N. Date 4-12-82

Classifier E.P.N. Date 4-12-82

Reviewer Date _____

Calculator Date _____

mation is recorded on forms that are separate from the record cards. The structure and appearance of the form will vary from state to state. Ask the office personnel for help. Usually the forms will be grouped by year and by type of property, e.g., commercial, residential, etc.

Many tax assessor offices maintain a file of properties that have been sold within their jurisdiction. Others flag these on the tax maps. Find a form for each of your comparables that indicates the amount and date of the sale. Use only those that have been sold within the past one to two years. The more recent the better, *but do not use those that are more recent than the tax year for which you plan to appeal.* Record the data on your form. If there are no sales data available in the tax office, contact a Realtor friend or someone who is a real estate appraiser. Ask him to help you gather the information that you need.

Another source of sales information is the county clerk's office. There you will find a copy of a deed showing the sales price for each property.

To locate the deed, you will need to access the grantee index. Usually, this index consists of a series of books that are arranged by year or years with the information listed in alphabetical order by grantee name (the person(s) who bought or now owns the property).

Locate the grantee's name in the index. Opposite his/her name(s) you will find the date that the title was transferred, and the deed book number and page number on which you can locate a copy of the deed. Find the deed book and record the date and sales price. Be sure to look for any information that indicates that the sale might have included personal property (such as furniture, etc.).

If it does, you must exclude that amount from the sales price to make your property comparable with it. In addition, check to be sure that the deed is for your comparable (the same lot and block number.) Sometimes the grantee will have purchased other properties. You must be positive that you have identified the correct one.

6. *Take pictures of your property and the three best comparables.*

For the most part, this makes your presentation look a little more professional and thorough. If you don't have a camera or don't want to bother taking the pictures, your presentation will not significantly suffer from an absence of photos.

7. *Prepare an analysis of your tax challenge research.*

Remember that there are four main reasons to challenge your property tax: a misvalued property, an illegal assessment, an unequal assessment, and mechanical errors. Carefully analyze the information you've collected to look for errors in each of these areas.

First, look at the information you've collected about your property and your comparables to see if you can make a case that your home is overassessed compared to similar properties. Use the blank forms provided in Appendix B and complete them.

Select the three comparables that are most favorable to your case (those that have a lower tax and assessed value) and record all information on a blank analysis form (see Appendix B). Use the examples on the following pages to help you record the proper data.

RESIDENTIAL MARKET ANALYSIS APPROACH

This approach consists of obtaining information on the sales of three similar homes located as close to the subject property (yours) as is possible. The sales prices of these homes are then adjusted to determine a fair market value for the subject (your) property.

The type of information you should gather to complete this analysis is shown below:

1. Location (this should be similar to the subject's—within a few blocks whenever possible)
2. Style (for example, whether the comparables are two-story, ranch, split-level, colonial, etc. —the style should be similar to the subject's)
3. Basement (finished or unfinished)
4. Size (the square feet of living area should be as close in size to the subject property's as possible)
5. Number of bedrooms
6. Number of bathrooms
7. Central air-conditioning
8. Fireplaces
9. Garage capacity (one, two, or more cars)

Enter all appropriate data on the blank forms provided. Use the sample on page 97 to guide you in entering the data.

For items 1 and 2, it is important that the comparables be located near the subject property and have a similar design and style. A dollar adjustment for these elements is difficult to prove.

Each of the items from 6 through 9 has a value in the marketplace. You will assign a value and make adjustments for each one relative to the subject property. Area Realtors and local appraisers will be able to supply you with standard value ranges for these adjustments because they use them for bank loans and other types of appraisals.

Always adjust (downward or upward) the value of the comparables relative to the subject property (yours).

The dollar figures on page 97 are for this example only. They may not be valid for your area. Consult a Realtor or appraiser for the current figures for your area.

Guide to Entering Data on the Market Analysis Form

Item	Source/Description
Property Address	Property record card or field research.
Distance to Subject	Approximate distance from your property, e.g., two blocks, one mile.
Sales Price	Obtained from Realtor, records in tax office, or valuation company.
Price/Liv. Area S/F	The sales price divided by the total square footage as shown under "Living Area S/F."
Source of Data	MLS = Multiple Listing Service—see your Realtor.
Date of Sale	If the market has been level during the period, no adjustment is needed.
Living Area S/F	Property record card, measurement, or construction office.
Location	The quality of the location.
Site/View	Land size or dimensions from property record card.
Design and Appeal	Type of design.

Item	Source/Description
Type of Construction	Frame, brick, stone, etc.
Age	Age of improvements from property record card.
Condition	Subjective opinion.
Room Count	Property record card.
Basement	Property record card.
Garage/Carport	Property record card or inspection.
Porch/Patio	Property record card or inspection.
Other	Make adjustments based on list provided on page 97 for major amenities.
Net Adj.—Total	Add the figures under the column labeled "Adj. +/−."
Indicated Value	Add the "Net adj.—total" figure to the "Sales Price."
Comments	Comment on the significant differences between the three comparables and the subject property.
Indicated Value by Market Data Analysis	Select a figure using the three indicated values. If one comparable is very close to the subject in most respects, choose a value slightly above it. Never choose a value below the lowest value.
Value per S/F	Divide the "Indicated Value by Market Data Analysis" figure by the "Living Area S/F" of the subject. Again, the figure used should be slightly above the lowest figure shown for "Price/Liv. Area S/F."

RESIDENTIAL MARKET DATA ANALYSIS

	Subject	Comp. #1		Comp. #2		Comp. #3	
Property Address	1313 Reed	1223 Reed		317 Manor		1306 Mason	
Distance to Subj.		w/in 1 block		w/in 4 blocks		w/in 5 blocks	
Sales Price	$185,425*	$170,500		$174,500		$169,500	
Price/Liv. Area S/F	$77.26	$71.04		$69.80		$72.12	
Source of Data	Assessor	MLS		MLS		MLS	
	Descrip.	**Descrip.**	**Adj. ±**	**Descrip.**	**Adj. ±**	**Descrip.**	**Adj. ±**
Date of Sale and Adjustment/Time	1-1-88	4-12-88		12-20-87		10-13-87	
Living Area S/F	2,400	2,400		2,500	−1000	2,350	+500
Location	Good	Good		Good		Good	
Site/View	1 acre	1 acre		1 acre		1 acre	
Design and Appeal	2 story	2 story		2 story		2 story	
Quality/Constr.	Brick	Brick		Brick		Brick	
Age	25	24		23		26	
Condition	Average	Average		Average		Average	
Room Count							
Total	8	9		7		8	
Bedrooms	4	4		4		4	
Baths	2½	2½		2	+1000	1½	+1500
Basement							
Finished						Yes	−3500
Unfinished	Yes	Yes		Yes			
Garage/Carport	2 car att	2 car att		3 car att	−2000	1 car att	+2000
Porch/Patio	Deck	Patio		Deck		Porch	+500
Other							
Swimming Pool							
Fireplace	Yes	None	+1200	Yes		Yes	
Kitchen Equip.							
Remodeling							
Air-conditioning							
			±		±		±
Net Adj.—Total			+1200		−2000		+1000
Indicated Value		$171,700		$172,500		$170,500	

Comments: All sales are similar in location and style and indicate a narrow adjusted-value range. Sale #1 is nearest the subject in location and size. Sale #2 is slightly larger, indicating a lower s/f value. Sale #3 is slightly smaller, indicating a higher s/f value. All sales were given equal consideration to arrive at a final value estimate.

Indicated Value by Market Data Analysis $172,000
or $71.66 per S/F

* The Sales Price and Price/Living Area for the subject are values set by the assessor, not by the actual sale of the subject. In this column, Sales Price is really the market value set by the assessor.

RESIDENTIAL EQUITY ANALYSIS APPROACH

This approach entails obtaining comparables for three homes that are located near the subject (your) property. If you are not using the market analysis approach with this approach, i.e., if you're using only the equity analysis method in your challenge, these homes do not have to have sold recently. If you are using both methods, obtain sales *and* assessment data for each comparable. Assessment information and property record cards are needed for all comparables and the subject. Try to obtain them from the tax assessor's office. If you are unable to do so, you may have to measure the properties yourself or talk to the owners to gather the needed data. You can also visit the local construction/engineer's or planning office to obtain square-footage figures and information about improvements or amenities.

Adjust the values of the three comparables relative to the subject property to arrive at an equitable assessment for your property. Make adjustments for the same items shown on the market analysis approach, e.g., size, baths, fireplaces, garages, air-conditioning, etc. Obtain current adjustment figures from a local Realtor or appraiser.

Use the blank equity analysis form in Appendix B to record this information, and use the two examples on the following pages as guides for completing the form. Remember that the adjustments shown are for examples only and are not representative of your area. You must research the appropriate dollar adjustments in use in your area.

Analysis and Reconciliation

All comparables are similar in location, style, age, and construction, and they have all received a similar

RESIDENTIAL EQUITY ANALYSIS—EXAMPLE #1

	Subject	Comp. #1	Comp. #2	Comp. #3
Property Address	1003 Cypress	810 Pearson	1013 Holly	1123 Brentle
Distance to Subj.		w/in 3 blocks	w/in 1 block	w/in 4 blocks
Assessed Value A/V	$24,998	$20,665	$20,286	$21,504
A/V Liv. Area S/F	$17.85	$14.76	$14.59	$15.23
Source of Data	Inspection	Assessor	Assessor	Assessor

	Descrip.	Descrip.	Adj. ±	Descrip.	Adj. ±	Descrip.	Adj. ±
Date of Sale and Adjustment/Time	1-1-88	1-1-88		1-1-88		1-1-88	
Living Area S/F	1,400	1,400		1,390		1,412	
Location	Average	Average		Average		Average	
Site/View	65 x 130	65 x 130		62 x 132		70 x 126	
Design and Appeal	Ranch	Ranch		Ranch		Ranch	
Quality/Constr.	Frame	Frame		Frame		Fr. w/brick	− 300
Age	25	25		24		28	
Condition	Average	Average		Average		Average	
Room Count							
Total	6	6		6		6	
Bedrooms	3	3		3		3	
Baths	1½	1	+ 333	1½		2½	− 500
Basement							
Finished	Slab	Slab		Slab		Slab	
Unfinished							
Garage/Carport	2 car det	2 car det		1 car det	+ 666	2 car det	
Porch/Patio	Patio	Patio		Patio		Patio	
Other							
Swimming Pool							
Fireplace	Yes	Yes		Yes		None	+ 400
Kitchen Equip.							
Remodeling							
Air-conditioning	Central	Central		Central		Central	
			±		±		±
Net Adj.—Total			+ 333		+ 666		− 400
Indicated Value		$20,998		$20,952		$21,104	

Comments: All 3 comparables are similar tract-type homes in the same subdivision as the subject. Minimal adjustments were required.

Indicated Assessed Valuation by Equity Analaysis $21,000
or $15.00 per S/F

* In this area, homes are assessed at one-third of market value. Therefore, all adjustments are at one-third of full value.

RESIDENTIAL EQUITY ANALYSIS—EXAMPLE #2

	Subject	Comp. #1	Comp. #2	Comp. #3
Name:	CASH	SMITH	JONES	JOHNSON
Address:	14 MAIN ST TOWER, NJ	27 MAIN ST TOWER, NJ	6 N. VINE TOWER, NJ	175 W. VIEW TOWER, NJ
Bldg. Assmt.:	$124,300	$116,900	$111,000	$110,000
S/F L/A:	2448	2378	2384	2526
A/V per S/F:	$50.78	$49.79	$46.56	$43.55
Construction	FRAME	FRAME	FAME	FRAME
Style:	2-STORY	2-STORY	2-STORY	2-STORY
Age:	1978	1978	1978	1978
Garage A/V:	$5,500	$6,300 (−$800)	5,900 (−$400)	$6,600 (−$900)
Driveway	GRAVEL	ASPHALT (−$2,900)	GRAVEL ($0)	GRAVEL ($0)
Other Amenities:	$25,257	$31,201 (−$5,944)	$26,327 (−$1,070)	$21,914 (+$3,343)
Total Adj.:	—	MINUS (−$9,644)	MINUS (−$1,470)	PLUS (+$2,443)
Adjusted Value:	—	$107,256	$109,530	$112,443
Adjd. S/F Value:	—	$45.10	$45.94	$44.51

degree of care and maintenance. Each comparable has some degree of similarity to the subject, with comparable #2 having the least value adjustments; they are all fairly similar in size. Based on this analysis, and considering all factors that affect value, an indicated fair and equitable building assessment for the subject would be:

$110,000 or $44.93 per S/F

Guide to Entries on the Equity Analysis Form

Item	Source/Description
Property Address	Property record card.
Distance to Subj.	Estimate the distance from the subject property, e.g., two blocks, one mile, etc.

Assessed Value A/V	Shown on the property record card or on the tax list.
Source of Data	Indicate where you got the data.
Date of Sale	Where no sale has taken place, indicate the current date.
Living Area S/F	Property record card or measurement in square feet.
Location	The quality of the location.
Site/View	Measurements of the land from record card.
Design and Appeal	The style of the improvements.
Quality/Constr.	The type and quality of construction.
Age	The age of the improvements from the property record card.
Condition	A subjective opinion.
Room Count	Property record card.
Basement	Property record card.
Garage/Carport	Property record card.
Porch/Patio	Property record card.
Other	Indicate the type of amenity and the adjustment therefor.
Net Adj.—Total	Add the figures under the column "Adj. +/−."
Indicated Value	Add the "Net Adj.—Total" figure to the "Assessed Value"
Comments	Enter comments relative to the similarity or differences between the subject and comparables.
Indicated Assessed Valuation by Equity Analysis	Using the indicated values that you calculated, select a value at which you want the subject property to be assessed. Always select a value higher than the lowest indicated

Item	Source/Description
	value shown and nearest the property that is most like the subject.
Value per S/F	Divide the "Indicated Assessed Value by Equity Analysis" by the "Living Area S/F" of the subject property.

CHECK FOR IMPROPER ASSESSMENTS AND RECORD ERRORS

Now that you've examined the possibility of an overassessment on your property, you should look at whether or not there are any problems with an illegal assessment, an unequal assessment, or record errors.

Let's look first at illegal assessments. Review the list in Chapter 6 for any areas that you may challenge. For example, check to see if your assessment is higher than the legal percentage, or higher than the sales-assessment ratio (see Chapter 6 for more information), or if your property is classified as other than a residential property and that it is in the proper sub-category when your state has this classification method.

Now look for an unequal assessment, also as described in Chapter 6. Here you are looking for an assessment higher than market value. Or, you may recently have purchased your property for less than the assessed value. Look for these situations and write them down.

Next, search for errors on your property record card. Check in the assessor's manual to verify that the correct factors were used. Check every calculation shown on your record card. Look for other conditions, such as those highlighted on the following two pages.

SAMPLE ONLY (not complete)

PROPERTY RECORD CARD

Township _TAXMANIA_   Taxing District _UP_   Section or Plat _____   Block _17_   Lot _4_

Property Address _16 W. MAIN ST._   Property Class _R_

Owner Name _JOHN & MARY JONES_

Owner Address _SAME_

Property Description:

     ENGLEWOOD SUB·DIVISION

     CORNER LOT

Assessment Record

Yr	Land	3420
	Bldgs	19073
	Total	22493

Property Factors

Topography	Improvements	Streets	District
Level _____	City Wtr. _X_	Pvd. _X_	Impr. _X_
High _____	Sewer _X_	Unimp. _____	Stat. _____
Low _____	Gas _____	Sidwlk. _X_	Decl. _____
Rolling _X_	Elect. _X_		Blight _____
Swampy _____	All util. _____		

Building Permits

Date	Number	Amount	Purpose
8/89	1234	$3500	DECK

Land Value Computations

Frontage	Depth	Unit Value	Depth Factor	Act. Value	True Value	Assessed Value
120	75	50	1-14	57	6840	

	True Value	Assessed Value
Total Land Value	6840	3420
Total Bldg Value	38146	19073
Total Value—Bldgs and Land		22493

SUMMARY

Remember that details are important when compiling the data you will use for your tax appeal. Be sure to double-check your figures.

Researching your appeal is the most important part of preparing your tax appeal case. You must proceed carefully and probe all possible areas for tax relief. If you don't find a problem, rest assured that the assessor won't bring any to your attention.

Keep complete lists of anything you find. Compile information together on one record. That way you won't overlook anything at appeal time.

Use the checklist in Appendix A so that you don't overlook any important items to examine. It is vital that you do a thorough job of analysis before you present your appeal.

CHECK FOR ERRORS SUCH AS THESE:

CHECK THE PROPERTY FACTORS
Are they accurate?

CHECK THE DEPTH FACTOR USED
Look it up in the assessor's manual.

CHECK THE UNIT VALUE
Is it fair compared to comparable sites?

CHECK THE LAND DIMENSIONS
Are they correct?

CHECK THE COMPUTATIONS
Were the calculations done accurately, e.g., 1.14 x $50 = $57 x 120 = $6840.

CHECK THE ASSESSED VALUE
Was it calculated properly according to the assessor's manual? Is the assessed value 50 percent (or some other prescribed figure) per the requirement in your state?

SAMPLE ONLY (not complete)

CHECK THE DESCRIPTIVE COMMENTS
They are the basis for selecting value figures. Make certain that they accurately describe the property.

CHECK THE DESCRIPTIONS FOR ERRORS
A one-story house may show two or more stories on the record.

CHECK ALL FIGURES FOR ACCURACY
There may be entries for items that don't exist or the wrong factors may have been used.

BUILDING RECORD	

Occupancy
Vacant Lot _____
Building ___X___ Qty. _1_
Plumbing
Standard ___X___ Nonstand. ___
Baths 1 ___ 2 _X_ 3 ___ 4 ___
Kitchen _MODERN_
Laundry ___X___
Water Heater ___X___
Basement
Finished _____ Unfinished _FULL_
Heating & Air-conditioning
Central Air ___X___
Hot Water/Steam _____
Electric _____
Unit heaters _____
Oil Forced Air ___X___
Gas _____
Exterior Walls
Brick _____ Stone _____ Block ___
Frame _X_ Other _____
Floors   B   1   2   3
Concrete   X
Wood   ___   X   X   ___
Tile   ___ ___ ___ ___
Interior finish
Dry wall ___X___
Other _____
Unfinished _____
Nbr. of rooms   B   1   2   3
                 -    5   3
Other features
Fireplaces ___X___ (1)
Other _____

CHECK THE FIGURES HERE
Were the building dimensions calculated accurately?

[Diagram: building outline with dimensions 15, 22, 20, 50, 30, 26]

Dwelling Computations

	Unit	Amount
	1520 S/F	.30400
A/C		1050
Attic		
Garage		1700
Other		
Other		
Subtotal 1		33150
Grade factor		1.24
Subtotal 2		41106
Cty. factor		1.16
Repl. value		47683
Depreciation		20
True Value		38146

Age _1975_
Date _8/90_

CHECK THESE FIGURES
The percentage used for depreciation may be inaccurate or may be calculated incorrectly.

CHAPTER 8

·

Key Points to Remember in Preparing Your Appeal

• You are trying to gather data that will show the lowest valid assessed value for your property. Therefore, always look for comparables with lower assessed values and/or market values than your property.

• Market value is the best indicator of value. Thus, if you use this approach and any other approach, such as cost or equity, more weight will be given to the conclusions reached using the market approach.

• By presenting facts about cost, market, or equity, your objective is to use them to prove that the value of your property is lower than the value shown on the property record card (the value on which your taxes are calculated). Always select the approach or approaches that show the value of your property in the most *unfavorable* light (i.e., the lowest value).

• When gathering sales data, make sure that the sale was a "usable" one. Transfers of convenience, sales that convey only part of the property, sales to or from charitable institutions, transactions where the full consideration was minimal, etc., are examples of "nonusable" sales. Avoid using them.

• With the equity approach, the comparables used must be within the same taxing jurisdiction as your (the subject) property. With the market data approach, this is not required. However, if you plan to submit data using both approaches, the comparables used should match. Therefore all must be within the same jurisdiction.

• In some states, the taxing jurisdiction can raise your assessed value as a result of your appeal, so be careful to analyze your data thoroughly before filing an appeal. Be certain that you aren't underassessed.

• If the data you gather does not support filing an appeal, examine your situation again the following year. You may find that you have a valid case at that time. Remember, many factors affect your assessed value.

• If your case goes to tax court, visit the court before you present your case to observe how the proceedings are conducted, what the members of the tax board talk about during the appeal of someone else's case, and to get a general feeling for what you can expect to happen when you appear.

• When preparing to negotiate with the tax assessor or members of the court, remember the rules of successful negotiating. Let the assessor make the first offer, and never say yes too quickly. Most libraries have helpful books that can help you improve your negotiating skills.

• The tax assessor is under a legal obligation to be fair and not litigious in providing you with information. The courts also view the homeowner as being competent to testify about the value of his residence, so don't lack confidence in presenting your case. You probably know even more about your house than does the tax assessor or the court.

• Before going to the tax court with an appeal, obtain a copy of the rules of the court by calling your local administrative offices.

• In a sense, the tax collection system is a political one. You should use this to your advantage. One way is to solicit the help of your neighbors where many may feel that they are unfairly taxed. There is strength in numbers. Consider making an appeal as a unified group. Share information with your neighbors. Read the newspapers and talk with your friends and neighbors about what is going on in the property tax arena.

· In some states, it is illegal to raise property taxes for a specified period after an addition or change to the property. In some jurisdictions, this period may last until the next revaluation is completed. If you've made significant changes or improvements, check with your assessor about the rules in your area.

CHAPTER 9

.

Presenting Your Appeal

PRESENTING YOUR CASE TO THE ASSESSOR

Contact your local assessor by telephone and arrange for a time to discuss your case. When you meet, present your case in a conversational, relaxed manner. Assessors are not to be feared. They are hardworking, busy people with strengths and weaknesses just like you.

Your meeting with the assessor should have an informal tone. Be relaxed, but direct and organized in your approach. You are there to say in effect, "I've been looking at my property tax situation. After gathering a substantial amount of information, doing a lot of checking, and organizing the facts that I've discovered, I feel my assessed value should be lowered. Here's why." There should be no confrontation, but merely a presentation of information by you that justifies your position.

It is important to your success that you be friendly, businesslike, and confident. Keep in mind that you know more about your property and your comparables than does the assessor. Be especially careful not to criticize the assessor for any errors you've found. Let the facts speak for themselves.

How you present your data is a matter of personal style and preference. Many experts find that an informal but organized approach is best. This will enable you to control the tone and direction of the discussion and avoid missing any important points that you want to cover. Have a general sequence in mind of what you intend to discuss. Begin with an overview statement, such as, "I have a market analysis, some questions I'd like to ask, and some facts to review that will illustrate why I believe that my taxes are too high. Shall we begin with the set of questions?" This approach gives the assessor a feel for the direction you wish to take, yet it allows you to control the sequence of your presentation. Beginning with a series of questions is nonthreatening and lets you both relax and break the ice.

Next, discuss any discrepancies or errors that you found. For example, if the depreciation factor assigned to the subject property (your home) is less than that for your comparables, you could bring this to the assessor's attention and inquire as to the reasons for the difference. To illustrate, let's say that your home shows a depreciation factor on the property record card of 5 percent while 15 percent was used for your comparables. If all properties are the same age, construction, and condition, your neighbors are getting better tax treatment than you are. If the cost of your house on the property record card was $125,000 with a 5-percent depreciation factor, the value used for taxes would be 95 percent of $125,000 or $118,750. For the sake of illustration, let's say that one of your comparables has the same cost as yours or $125,000, but the depreciation factor applied is 15 percent. The assessed value would be $125,000 multiplied by 85 percent or $106,250. Thus, you are paying taxes on the difference ($118,750 minus $106,250, or $12,500) when you shouldn't be. Here is where you might want to produce good photographs of the comparable homes to convince the assessor that they all are in the same condition, and that you are being overtaxed.

If you have found other factors that have an impact on the assessed value, such as math errors, differences in depreciation, etc., that will lower your assessed value, you should review them with the assessor. Your purpose is to demonstrate how the cost valuation used on the property record card is incorrect. A reduction in this value will lower your tax obligation.

Finally, you should present your market analysis and/or equity analysis data. You could briefly highlight how you arrived at the final values and conclude with the value at which you believe your property should be assessed. Suggesting—and supporting—the value you want is very important. Your analysis will support your conclusion of value and you need to point this out to your assessor. To not suggest a value would allow the assessor to form his or her own conclusion—that might not be as satisfactory for you.

Whenever you make an appeal, keep in mind that the value of a property is partly subjective. It is an opinion that is supported by facts, but there can still be differences of opinion about those facts. You may not get total agreement from the assessor as to the value you have established.

Usually the assessor will tell you that he or she will look at your records and the data you presented and call you in a few days with an opinion. Rarely will a decision be given on the spot, even if one could be given. Don't let that bother you. It's routine.

When you and the assessor get back together, the assessor may offer to settle on a value that is higher than your facts indicate. You can try to negotiate further, but if you are unable to convince him to accept your figure, you must decide whether or not to settle for his higher valuation. Your alternative is to proceed to the local review board. It might be better to accept a slightly higher valuation than to risk an even worse settlement later.

The assessor will usually prefer to make a settlement on his level than to have to justify the assessment in the presence of his superiors in a courtroom atmosphere at the review board hearing. You can always make another appeal the following year and perhaps achieve a more satisfactory valuation.

If you accept the decision, you will receive a notice of a reduction in assessed value within a week or two.

If the assessor's decision is unfavorable and you don't want to accept it, plan to file a formal appeal. The procedure for a formal appeal is described later in this chapter.

If you settle and have a mortgage, your mortgage company will be notified that your tax bill has been reduced. They then will send you a statement that may give you the option of a reduced monthly payment (mortgage payment and tax payment combined) or of the excess dollars collected being placed in an escrow account to be applied toward later tax increases.

PRESENTING YOUR CASE TO THE REVIEW BOARD

The review board usually consists of three to five people who, depending on the state you are in, are either appointed or elected to the board. Often they are people with varied backgrounds, but many have been or are involved in the real estate field in one way or another, or serve in some other government capacity.

There may be two ways in which to present your case to the assessment review board:

1. Submission of a grievance statement along with supporting documents may be all that is required to present the case. No appearance is necessary.
2. The property owner and/or a designated person may be permitted to support the written statement before the board. This individual may be a property tax attorney or a property tax consultant. A consultant may act as an expert witness, but may not always represent the client in a legal capacity. A lawyer may represent the client *and* act as an expert witness. Check your local laws by calling the tax administration office.

If you represent yourself at the review board hearing, you may want to prepare presentation displays for use before the review board. This is a matter of personal style and choice. You may, of course, feel more comfortable just using your documentation to speak from. If so, be sure you furnish the board with a copy to refer to while you present your facts.

The board, in most instances, will not make its decision immediately in your presence. Having heard the evidence and read the documents submitted, it may proceed to the next case and subsequently meet separately and resolve all cases. Once a decision is reached, the board will direct the assessor to make whatever changes are determined. Most likely the grievant (that's you) will not be notified directly of the board's action. These results can be found out from the assessor's office.

You have an opportunity once each year to file your appeal. If you miss that chance, you must wait until the following year to make a challenge for any tax relief.

Therefore, you should check with the tax assessor's office as to when the filing period is.

After all complaints are heard, the final assessment roll must be completed. It may again be open for public inspection, but taxpayers can no longer file grievances. This public inspection has no particular significance other than to let the public be aware of the final assessed values.

JUDICIAL REVIEW

Once the results of the grievance at the local level are learned, a determination must be made whether or not you are satisfied with the decision. If you are not, you may carry the case to a higher court. This may be a special agency, a tax court, or an appeals court. In any case, this group has the power to sustain or overturn an assessment that was locally made.

As with the original grievance procedure, there is a limited time for filing an appeal. This information is accessible through your state's real property tax laws or the Commerce Clearing House Tax Guide.

Whenever you are considering an appeal to a higher court, you should consult with a qualified property tax attorney to review your case and advise you whether or not a further appeal is worthwhile. At this level, due to the expense of legal counsel, you should be sure that you have a strong case. Usually, however, attorneys work on a contingency basis, charging a fee only if they win your case.

If you are requesting a reduction of your taxes of at least 10 percent, you may want to proceed. This is purely a judgment call and legal counsel is advised.

CHAPTER 10

.

Sample Cases

SINGLE FAMILY HOUSE

To be sure that you thoroughly understand what must be done to prepare a successful appeal, let's examine the property tax situation of John and Mary Doe. They are typical homeowners who live in Middletown, USA. They think that their property taxes are too high, but they know they will have to prove it to the local tax authorities. So they decide to gather the appropriate information and prepare an appeal. Here is what they did.

John and Mary live in a development of about 125 homes that have a range of market values from $75,000 to $106,000. About six months ago, they considered selling their house, but then decided to remain there for another few years. At that time, they asked a local Realtor to prepare a market study to establish a fair market price for their home. (Keep in mind that a market study, by a real estate salesperson, or an appraisal, by an independent appraiser, employs comparables to estimate the approximate value of a property.) The results of her study indicated that a price of $89,500 would be about right for their property. Not much has changed in the real estate marketplace since that time.

John and Mary know of a house in the next block that sold for $82,000 about two months ago. The taxes on that property are $955 per year. The house is similar to theirs: it is the same style, a ranch with a full basement, three bedrooms, one and a half baths, 1,600 square feet of living space with a double garage.

The tax on their property is $1,265 per year. John and Mary don't understand why they are paying so much more in taxes, but they plan to find out by doing a market analysis and by examining the records for their property in the Middletown tax assessor's office.

John began by driving around the neighborhood to locate some comparable properties. In identifying them, he kept in mind that they had to be within a few blocks of his property, had to be of similar style, age, and size, and had to have sold within the last year or so.

He found six houses that he thought would meet these criteria and wrote a brief description of each one. Here they are:

Comparable #1: 3BR ranch, 1-car attached garage, fenced yard, wood siding, asphalt roof, paved driveway, small deck in back. Address—86 Mill Ave.

Comparable #2: 3BR ranch, 1-car attached garage, brick construction, asphalt roof, paved driveway, air-conditioning. Address—107 Hemlock.

Comparable #3: 3BR ranch with 1-car attached garage, aluminum siding, asphalt-shingle roof, cement driveway, fireplace. Owner—Herman; Address—156 Hemlock.

Comparable #4: 3BR ranch, 1-car attached garage, wood siding, stone driveway, nice landscaping, window air conditioner, asphalt roof. Address—4 Maple Ave.

Comparable #5: 3BR with storage shed, 1-car attached garage, paved driveway, aluminum siding, fenced yard in back, fireplace, deck. Address—217 Furnace Road.

Comparable #6: 3BR ranch, wood siding with stone facing in front, fireplace, pool, paved driveway, asphalt roof, air-conditioning. Owner—Gibbs; Address —147 Palmer Terrace.

John gave this information to Mary, and she went to the Middletown assessor's office to gather more data. She located each of the properties on a tax list and then on a tax map. She obtained the lot and block numbers, confirmed the addresses and owners' names, the assessed values, the annual taxes, the property classifications, and she drew a sketch of each lot that included the dimensions.

Mary also searched for information about the sale of each of these properties. One of them, the house located at 147 Palmer Terrace, had been sold about three years ago. The house at 107 Hemlock had not been sold as John had thought.

Mary asked the assessor for a copy of her property record card. The assessor furnished it without any resistance. When she asked for the cards on the other properties, she was told that she could look at them, but couldn't have a copy. She took notes about the assessments, the size of the improvements, the number of bedrooms and baths, basements, etc.

When Mary got home, she and John reviewed the information that she had gathered. When Mary mentioned that one of the houses had not been sold as he had thought and that another was sold more than three years ago, John decided to look for another comparable to replace them. He remembered a house that was two miles away in another development that had been sold a year ago. He drove over to see it and wrote a description of it a few days later. The house had four bedrooms, a fireplace, air-conditioning, a paved driveway, about 2,000 square feet of living area, and was located on a corner lot.

Next, John and Mary filled out a market analysis form and completed an equity analysis as well. They decided that the last house that John researched was too far away and was substantially larger than theirs and the others. They felt the others would be better comparisons.

Mary contacted her Realtor friend and asked for some help with the cost-adjustment factors. She introduced Mary to an appraiser with whom she does business. He helped Mary with the data that she needed to do the market analysis and to check out the property record card calculations (computations and the adjustments for the type of construction, the pavement on the driveway, the deck, plumbing, heating, electrical, etc.). Note: If Mary didn't know any Realtors, she could get adjustment figures from a tax assessor or check her library for any *current* adjustment data. Usually, Realtors will be helpful because they are hoping for a listing and/or subsequent sale, or a reference for being helpful. Mary also went back to the assessor's office and reviewed the state manual to learn more about the cost figures that were used on the record card. Once she had checked a few of the figures on the card against the state manual, she felt more confident. Mary found that she was able to verify properly the sources of the factors used and the accuracy of the assessor's computations.

The results of her verifications and the two analysis forms are on the following pages. She and John used this information for their discussion with the assessor. Both forms show an "indicated value by market data analysis" with comments and a value per square foot. These figures are used to demonstrate the value that Mary and John believe should be established for their property. The adjustments demonstrate how and why the concluded value was derived. All of these data are used to persuade the tax assessor to change the value.

John and Mary prepared a brief outline of what they wanted to review with the assessor. They scheduled a meeting and went over the facts. Because they had taken the time and made the effort to analyze the data properly, they were successful in reducing their taxes to $1,005 per year. That's a saving of $260 each year. Their time was well spent!

Questions You Might Ask About This Case:

1. Were the results of the market study done by the Realtor important in this appeal?

Not really. The potential sales price, although derived by the Realtor using comparables, is significant only as another opinion as to value. It was an estimate of the price at which to list the property. It may or may not sell at that price. If you can demonstrate a lower market value with other comparables and they are valid ones, you should use them. Be prepared, however, to defend your selection of comparables.

2. What significance did the house that sold for $82,000 have in this case?

It got the Does thinking about comparable properties and the fact that a house similar to theirs was being taxed less than their home. This is the value of doing an equity analysis.

3. Why should the Does reject the additional comparable found by John in favor of the others?

It was larger by 25 percent. It was two miles away in a different development. By using comparables that were closer and in their own development, they were able to present a stronger case. The proximity of the comparables to your residence is very important in establishing value.

4. Why do an equity analysis when market value is the best approach to value?

An equity analysis, in those states that allow its use, is a good indication that a property is being over-taxed. It breaks down the value on a square-footage basis for ease of comparison. If the comparables used are the same as those used in the market analysis, and they should be, your case is substantially strengthened because you are demonstrating in two ways that your residence is overtaxed.

5. Why is it important to check out the computations and factors used by the assessor on the property record card?

Cost is a recognized approach to value. If the figures used to assess your property yield a result that shows you should be taxed less, it may be the best approach to use in your case. Errors in computation or in the selection of adjustment factors can save you lots of money if you discover them.

CONDOMINIUM OR TOWN HOUSE

If your residence is a condominium or town house and you want to attempt to reduce your property taxes, your approach will be similar in most respects to what we have already discussed. It will be different in the sense that the analysis of comparable proper-ties takes on a different form. You may want to use a sales ratio approach. In effect, you'll be comparing the assessed value to the sales price for condomin-iums or town houses, similar to yours, that have been sold within the last year or so. For example, suppose

HOW TO LOWER YOUR PROPERTY TAXES

RESIDENTIAL MARKET DATA ANALYSIS

	Subject	Comp. #1		Comp. #2		Comp. #3	
Property Address	165 Mill Ave	86 Mill Ave		156 Hemlock		217 Furnace	
Distance to Subj.		w/in 1½ blocks		w/in 2 block		w/in 4 blocks	
Sales Price	$92,500*	$82,000		$86,900		$87,000	
Price/Liv. Area S/F	$56.06	$51.25		$51.12		$52.41	
Source of Data	Assessor	MLS		REDI		MLS	
	Descrip.	**Descrip.**	**Adj. ±**	**Descrip.**	**Adj. ±**	**Descrip.**	**Adj. ±**
Date of Sale and Adjustment/Time	6-1-88	10-6-88		5-1-88		11-15-88	
Living Area S/F	1,650	1,600	+ 500	1,700	− 500	1,660	− 100
Location	Good	Good		Good		Good	
Site/View	100 x 165	98 x 164		100 x 166		97 x 167	
Design and Appeal	1 story rnch	1 sty rch		1 sty rch		1 sty rch	
Quality/Constr.	Frame	Frame		Frame		Fr. & Brk.	− 780
Age	7	8		7		6	
Condition	Average	Average		Average		Average	
Room Count							
Total	7	7		8		7	
Bedrooms	3	3		3		3	
Baths	1½	1½		2	− 360	1½	
Basement							
Finished				Full	− 1860	Full	− 1822
Unfinished	Full	Full					
Garage/Carport	1 car att	1 car att		1 car att		1 car att	
Porch/Patio	Deck	Deck		Deck	+ 322	Deck	
Other							
Swimming Pool							
Fireplace				Yes	− 1100	Yes	− 1100
Kitchen Equip.							
Remodeling							
Air-conditioning							
Fin. Concessions		FHA		FHA		FHA	
			±		±		±
Net Adj.—Total			+ 500		− 3498		− 3802
Indicated Value		$82,500		$83,402		$83,198	

Comments: All 3 comparables are similar in terms of location, size, and age. Comp. #1 is nearest the subject in location. Comp. #2 is slightly larger resulting in a lower S/F value, and it has more adjustments. Comp. #3 is farthest away from the subject. Considering all factors that affect value, an indicated fair and final value for the subject would be

Indicated Value by Market Data Analysis **$83,200**
or $50.42 per S/F

* Market value determined by assessor estimate, not by actual sale.

RESIDENTIAL EQUITY ANALYSIS

	Subject	Comp. #1		Comp. #2		Comp. #3	
Property Address	165 Mill Ave	86 Mill Ave		156 Hemlock		217 Furnace	
Distance to Subj.		w/in 1½ blocks		w/in 2 block		w/in 4 blocks	
Assessed Value A/V	$46,250	$40,100		$41,326		$40,775	
A/V Liv. Area S/F	$28.03	$25.06		$24.31		$24.56	
Source of Data	Assessor	Assessor		Assessor		Assessor	
	Descrip.	**Descrip.**	**Adj. ±**	**Descrip.**	**Adj. ±**	**Descrip.**	**Adj. ±**
Date of Sale and Adjustment/Time							
Living Area S/F	1,650	1,600	+ 250	1,700	− 250	1,660	− 50
Location	Good	Good		Good		Good	
Site/View	100 x 165	98 x 164		100 x 166		97 x 167	
Design and Appeal	1 sty ranch	1 sty rch		1 sty rch		1 sty rch	
Quality/Constr.	Frame	Frame		Frame		Fr. & Brick	− 390
Age	7	8		7		6	
Condition	Average	Average		Average		Average	
Room Count							
Total	7	7		8		7	
Bedrooms	3	3		3		3	
Baths	1½	1½		2	− 180	1½	
Basement							
Finished				Full	− 930	Full	− 911
Unfinished	Full	Full					
Garage/Carport	1 car att	1 car att		1 car att		1 car att	
Porch/Patio	Deck	Deck		None	+ 161	Deck	
Other							
Swimming Pool							
Fireplace	None	None		Yes	− 550	Yes	− 550
Kitchen Equip.							
Remodeling							
Air-conditioning	Central	Central		Central		Central	
			±		±		±
Net Adj.—Total			+ 250		− 1749		− 1901
Indicated Value		$40,350		$39,577		$38,874	

Comments: All comparables are similar in construction and age and are located in the same subdivision within 4 blocks of each other. Based on this analysis, an indicated fair and equitable assessment value for the subject would be:

Indicated Assessed Valuation by Equity Analysis $40,100
or $24.30 per S/F

* This taxing district is assessed at one-half of market value. All adjustments therefore, are at one-half of full value.

you own Model A in a condominium development. You will have to identify other Model A units in that development that have sold within the last year. Then you will calculate the ratio of the assessed value for each one to its sales price. Next you will compute an average for all of the comparables that you use in the study.

Of course, you can effectively use the standard market approach discussed in earlier sections to prove your case. Select three comparable sales in your development, make adjustments, calculate square footages, etc., and determine what the assessed value on your property should be. You may want to examine both approaches and decide which one presents your case in a more favorable light.

The sales ratio study that follows will illustrate the ratio method. Some of the key figures used in the study are explained below. A guide to interpreting and using the figures will appear in the pages that follow.

Explanation of Terms Used in the Sales Ratio Study

Block—The number assigned to the block shown on the tax map that represents the area in which the condominiums/town houses are located.

Lot—The lot number assigned to each individual condominium/town-house property as identified on the tax map.

1989 Assessed Value—Assessed value as determined by the tax assessor for tax purposes. Three figures are shown: one for the assessed value of the land, one for the improvements thereon (e.g., the condo building), and the sum or total of the two figures.

AV/SP—Assessed value (AV) divided by the sales price (SP).

No. of Sales—The number of sales included under the column.

SALES RATIO STUDY
VALLEYBROOK CONDOMINIUMS BLOCK 36

Lot	Year Built	1989 Assessed Value (Figs. in 1,000s)			Sales Price (Figs. in 1,000s)		Sales Date	Ratio AV/SP
		Land	Improv	Total	Model A	Model B		
5.05	1986	$71.3	$140.1	$211.4	$235.0		11/08/88	89.96%
5.08	1985	$75.9	$160.4	$236.3		$280.0	12/12/88	84.39%
5.17	1986	$75.0	$140.1	$215.1	$277.0		12/15/88	77.65%
5.18	1985	$75.0	$140.1	$215.1	$269.9		3/09/89	79.70%
5.21	1986	$75.9	$162.4	$238.3		$290.0	7/15/89	82.17%
5.23	1986	$75.0	$140.1	$215.1	$254.5		1/10/89	84.52%
5.45	1986	$75.0	$145.3	$220.3	$252.3		10/27/88	87.32%
5.54	1986	$75.0	$147.8	$222.8		$283.0	3/31/89	78.73%
5.56	1986	$75.9	$140.1	$216.0	$258.5		9/16/89	83.56%
Totals				$1990.4	$1547.2	$853.0		748.00%
No. of Sales				9	6	3		9
Mean Sales Price					$ 257.9	$284.3		
Mean Assessment				$ 221.2	$ 215.5	$232.5		
Mean Sales Ratio (AV/SP)					83.56%	81.78%		83.11%

Notes:

1. All units have a 2-car garage, basement, fireplace, 2 bedrooms, frame construction, and were built in 1985 & 1986.
2. Square footage of model A is 2161 and of model B is 2641.
3. Square-footage figures exclude garage and basement.
4. Only sales between 10/15/88 and 10/14/89 were included because those dates coincide with the figures used by the tax assessor for the tax year.

Mean Sales Price (avg. sales price)—Figure shown as "Totals" under the "Sales Price" column divided by the "No. of Sales" shown for that model.

Mean Assessment (avg. assessed value)—Sum of the figure shown under the heading, "1989 assessed value—Total" ($1990.4) and "Sales Price—Model A" ($1547.2) and Model B ($853.0) divided by the respective number of sales (9, 6, or 3) shown under each. For example, $1990.4 ÷ 9 = $221.2, or $1547.2 ÷ 6 = $215.5, etc.

Mean Sales Ratio—The figure(s) shown under the "Sales Price" column(s) that represents the "Mean Sales Price" divided into the figure that represents the "Mean Assessment." Under the "Ratio AV/SP" column, the "Mean Sales Ratio" is derived by dividing the number of sales shown into the "Totals" figure shown under that column. Thus, it is an average for both models added together.

Let's assume that the subject property in our example is located on lot 5.10, is a Model A unit, and has an assessed value of $221,000. It is similar in all respects to the units shown in the study. If we had purchased the unit for $258,500 on 1/15/89, and we applied the mean sales ratio to that figure, the assessed value should be about $216,000 ($258,500 × 83.56% or .8356 = $216,002.60). Thus, we would ask the assessor to lower our assessed value to that figure. If we had been living in the unit for several years, so that there had been no recent sale of the subject property, we could request a reduction to the "mean assessment" amount that we calculated in our study to be $215,500.

In either case, the amount of reduction in actual taxes paid would be small. The reduction in assessed value was minimal, only $5,000 to $5,500, and the tax rate, if it is assumed to be $1.05 per $100 of assessed value, would yield a savings of $52.50 or $57.75 per year, respectively. You will, however, enjoy this saving each year until another valuation is done in your community. The point is that our objective is to determine whether or not we are being taxed fairly and equitably. Here, we were close, but should still receive a small reduction. At least we know our situation.

In some states, an appeal may be made by the Condominium Association on behalf of the individual owners, provided that the condominium declaration allows for the association to appeal their taxes as a group when there is a majority vote to do so.

If this is the approach used, you should conduct a sales ratio study on another condominium development that is similar to yours and is located nearby. A comparison of the mean sales ratios for both developments should be done. The other development, not yours, should have the lowest ratios. This shows that your development is paying higher taxes based on a comparison between sales and assessed values. Be certain, however, that the square footages are similar between the developments and that there are no significant differences between the units in both developments.

For a cooperative (co-op) arrangement, where the Cooperative Association owns the building(s) and leases space to the shareholders of the association (the theoretical owners of each co-op apartment), a sales ratio study should be done to compare the entire building to another, similar co-op building in the same geographic area.

CHAPTER 11

.

Enjoying Your Win

If you have put forth the effort to properly analyze your property tax situation and you decided to appeal your taxes for valid reasons, congratulations are in order. You probably have won your appeal. You have beaten city hall—an accomplishment you may not ever have dreamed of or even thought possible.

Although you may have spent several hours looking for comparables, gathering data, and preparing and presenting your case, you should feel satisfaction in what you have achieved. And should you acquire another residence in the future, you now know enough about the property tax system to do it again.

In addition to feeling satisfied, you will be paid for your work for years to come by the tax reduction that you've won. It can add up to lots of dollars over the years.

Congratulations! Enjoy the fruits of your labor!

.

Checklist for Appealing Your Property Taxes

Have you prepared a market data analysis?   _____

- Your comparables are located in the same general area as the subject property and are similar in age and design   _____
- All comparables were sold within the last one to two years   _____
- You adjusted all amenities to the subject property   _____
- You used current figures for your area with which to make adjustments   _____
- All sales shown were "usable" ones   _____
- Your comparables have lower assessed values per square foot than the subject property   _____
- You concluded your analysis with a suggested value   _____
- Your suggested value is higher than the lowest comparable value   _____
- Your suggested value was closest to the adjusted value of the comparable with the least adjustments   _____

Have you prepared a cost analysis?   _____

- If current sales data aren't available, you used this approach to value   _____
- You used the current cost figures for your area when making cost adjustments   _____
- You sought the assistance of a competent appraiser or real estate person to obtain

cost values and to help you with your analysis _____

Have you prepared an equity analysis? _____

- You have checked to determine whether or not an equity analysis is acceptable in your state _____
- The comparables you used are within the same taxing jurisdiction _____
- If you use a market analysis, the comparables used in the equity analysis match those in the market analysis _____

Have you checked for an illegal assessment? _____

- Your property is assessed at more than the legal assessment _____
- Your property was not inspected by the assessor _____
- The assessor used the wrong approach to value your property _____
- Your assessment is higher than the state-issued sales-assessment ratio _____
- Your property is not assessed within the proper class _____
- A notice of increased assessment was not issued _____

Have you checked the personal exemptions to which you are entitled? _____

Have you checked for an unequal assessment? _____

- Your property is assessed at more than market value _____

Assessments on similar properties are lower than on your property   _____

• You recently purchased your property for less than the assessed value   _____

Have you checked for mathematical and mechanical errors in your tax records?   _____

• See pages 74–79 for areas you can check   _____

Have you determined that the depreciation used for your property was correct?   _____

To avoid a tax increase, have you checked that your property is not underassessed before filing your appeal?   _____

Have you organized your presentation for the discussion with your tax assessor so that it follows a logical sequence and concludes with a suggested value?   _____

APPENDIX B

.

Forms

RESIDENTIAL MARKET DATA ANALYSIS

	Subject	Comp. #1	Comp. #2	Comp. #3
Property Address	_____	_____	_____	_____
Distance to Subj.	_____	_____	_____	_____
Sales Price	$_____	$_____	$_____	$_____
Price/Liv. Area S/F	$_____	$_____	$_____	$_____
Source of Data	_____	_____	_____	_____

	Descrip.	Descrip.	Adj. ±	Descrip.	Adj. ±	Descrip.	Adj. ±
Date of Sale and Adjustment/Time							
Living Area S/F							
Location							
Site/View							
Design and Appeal							
Quality/Constr.							
Age							
Condition							
Room Count Total Bedrooms Baths							
Basement Finished Unfinished							
Garage/Carport							
Porch/Patio							
Other Swimming Pool Fireplace Kitchen Equip. Remodeling Air-conditioning							
			±		±		±
Net Adj.—Total							
Indicated Value		$_____		$_____		$_____	

Comments: _____

_____

_____

Indicated Value by Market Data Analysis . . . .$_____

or $_____ per S/F

RESIDENTIAL EQUITY ANALYSIS

	Subject	Comp. #1		Comp. #2		Comp. #3	
Property Address							
Distance to Subj.							
Assessed Value A/V	$	$		$		$	
A/V Liv. Area S/F	$	$		$		$	
Source of Data							
	Descrip.	Descrip.	Adj. ±	Descrip.	Adj. ±	Descrip.	Adj. ±
Date of Sale and Adjustment/Time							
Living Area S/F							
Location							
Site/View							
Design and Appeal							
Quality/Constr.							
Age							
Condition							
Room Count Total Bedrooms Baths							
Basement Finished Unfinished							
Garage/Carport							
Porch/Patio							
Other Swimming Pool Fireplace Kitchen Equip. Remodeling Air-conditioning							
			±		±		±
Net Adj.—Total							
Indicated Value		$		$		$	

Comments: _____

_____

_____

Indicated Assessed Valuation by Equity Analysis . . . .$_____

or $_____ per S/F

GLOSSARY

APPRAISED VALUE—The value of a property as determined by research and comparative data gathered by a real estate appraiser. It represents an opinion or estimate of a property's value.

APPROACHES TO VALUE—There are three generally accepted methods used to determine the value of a property: market data (actual sales prices paid for property), income (the net income a property generates from a lease or rental), and cost (the cost to replace or reproduce a structure, e.g., a house, using standard cost data supplied by a cost-research firm). A fourth method, the equity approach (a comparison of the assessed values on a square-footage basis), is recognized in some states.

Wherever possible, all approaches should be used to determine the value of a property for tax purposes. Since property values tend to change slowly, values arrived at by one method alone may not reflect the actual property value. Abnormal market conditions of short duration may bring about prices that do not really indicate the true value of a property. Likewise, abnormal construction costs or income conditions may also cause a distortion of the true value.

ASSESSED VALUE—An estimate as to the value of a property in the opinion of the tax assessor. The value determined may be based on full market value or a fraction thereof. The assessed value is used to calculate the amount of property tax due on a property.

ASSESSMENT RATIO—The ratio of assessed value to full market value. As an example, assume that a property sold for $80,000. If the assessed value is $40,000, the assessment ratio can be calculated by dividing the assessed value ($40,000) by the sales price ($80,000). The resulting ratio is 50 percent ($40,000/$80,000). An assessment ratio of 50 percent indicates that properties in the taxing municipality have an assessed value that is one-half (50%) of full market value.

The ratio may be defined either by statute (law) or by the relationship between assessed value and market value as determined by studies done by the taxing authorities.

COMPARABLES—Properties that have been sold and are used for comparison purposes in the assessment and appraisal processes.

DEPRECIATION—The loss in value from all causes in any structure. The loss may be due to physical depreciation (due to aging), functional obsolescence (loss over and above physical depreciation caused by factors within the subject property), or economic obsolescence (same as functional obsolescence, but outside the subject property).

The term does not apply to land, but only to the improvements thereon. Depreciation can be due to physical deterioration or functional or economic obsolescence.

FULL MARKET VALUE—The amount of money that would probably be arrived at through fair negotiations between a willing seller and a willing buyer, taking into consideration the uses to which the property may be put.

TAX ASSESSOR—The government official responsible for establishing the value of property for *ad valorem* tax purposes (a tax based solely upon value). He or she may be elected, appointed, or under civil service and may be known by many different names, such as evaluator, assessment commissioner, appraiser, or assessor. The assessor is responsible for discovering, listing, and valuing all taxable real and personal property within a taxing jurisdiction, such as a town, county, township, borough, parish, etc.

TAX COLLECTOR—A local-level government employee who is responsible for the distribution of tax bills to property owners within his taxing jurisdiction and the collection of the tax. This function may be carried out by the town clerk, but usually it is not done by the tax assessor.

TAX RATE—A rate that is applied to the assessed value of your property to determine the amount of property tax to be paid. It is calculated by dividing the budget (the total of the monies to be spent in three ways: bonded indebtedness, schools, and all other services) of a taxing municipality, less any anticipated revenues from non-property-tax sources, by the total assessed value of the assessment roll (all taxable properties). An individual value (assessed value) is multiplied by the rate to obtain an individual tax bill.

The tax rate can be expressed in dollars per $100 or $1,000 of assessed value or in millage (thousandths of a dollar).

REFERENCES

The Appraisal of Real Estate. American Institute of Real Estate Appraisers of the National Association of Realtors, 430 N. Michigan Ave., Chicago, IL 60611. Eighth edition, 1983.

Appraising the Single Family Residence. American Association of Real Estate Appraisers of the National Association of Realtors, 430 N. Michigan Ave., Chicago, IL 60611. 1985 printing.

Changing Times magazine, September 1988, Vol. 42, No. 9. Article entitled "Home Property Taxes: How to Fight Back."

Forbes magazine, November 3, 1986. Article entitled "Who Gets the Windfall?" by Laura Saunders.

Fundamentals of Real Estate Appraisal. Ventoto, William L., Jr., 4th Ed., 1983, revised 1987.

How to Appraise Your Own Home. Rhodes, Richard M., Delphi Books, 1980.

Money magazine, May 1990. Article entitled "Honey, I Shrunk the Property Taxes!" by Teresa Tritch.

New Jersey Superior Court Reports, Vol. 235. *Township of West Milford, Plaintiff-Respondent* v. *Gerald and Juanita Van Decker, Defendants-Appellants.* Decided June 21, 1989.

Property Assessment Valuation. A book by the International Association of Assessing Officers, 1313 E. Sixtieth Street, Chicago, IL 60637. Copyright 1977.

Real Estate Investment Planning, second issue, August
1987. Article entitled "A Growing Business: Lowering Property Tax Assessments." Published by
Prentice-Hall, Inc., Englewood Cliffs, NJ 07632.

INDEX

About the Author

Mr. Koenig is the owner of King Associates, a tax-consulting firm located in New Jersey. He assists property owners who are being taxed inequitably in reducing their property tax obligations. Prior to founding this firm, he was in middle management with a Fortune 100 company.

He has a New Jersey real estate license and is an active investor in real estate. He holds a B.S. degree in finance from Arizona State University, is a graduate of the U.S. Army Command & General Staff College, and attended law school at the University of Arizona.

His book has been written about in numerous newspapers, such as the *Seattle Times*, the *Boston Globe*, the *Bergen Record*, and many other publications throughout the U.S. It was also mentioned in an article in *Money* magazine and was discussed on the "Money Talk" program on the Financial News Network.